The World's Toughest Disney Quiz Book

Shaun Finnie

The World's Toughest Disney Quiz Book

1 3 5 7 9 10 8 6 4 2

First published by Lulu, 2012.

ISBN 978-1-4716-8753-2

For more info, a weekly blog and a free short story every month, visit www.shaunfinnie.com

For Jill

Introduction

So you think you're a Disney fan? You can reel off the names of the Seven Dwarfs without pausing for breath? You have Walt's birthday and the anniversary of Disneyland's opening day on your calendar along with your family's birthdays and your wedding anniversary? You spend all your vacation time at the theme parks and when you're not there you're planning your next visit?

Congratulations. You're a card-carrying, ear-wearing Disney geek.

But how well do you *really* know the wonderful world of Disney? The films, the theme parks, the TV shows. And what about the stage shows, the cruise ships, the cancelled projects? Or maybe even the video games, the comic books and the people who created all these things?

Still sure you know your Disney stuff?

Take the challenge or, better still, challenge your Disney-loving friends. Try The World's Toughest Disney Quiz Book. It's stuffed with a thousand questions and answers to test even the most ardent Disney fan's knowledge.

Could you be the ultimate Disney mastermind?

Question Set 1

1-1) What was the name of Pete's Dragon?

1-2) Which Disney character's middle name is Fauntleroy?

1-3) Which character was played in the Pirates of the Caribbean films by Keira Knightley?

1-4) Under what name did Mickey's dog Pluto originally appear?

1-5) Approximately how much did Disneyland cost to build when it opened?

1-6) Who was the voice of Esmeralda in Disney's 'The Hunchback of Notre Dame'?

1-7) What theme park did Disney plan for Long Beach, California?

1-8) What was the first Mickey Mouse short film to be made?

1-9) The stars of which abandoned Disney project from the 1940's (about small creatures sabotaging the British Royal Air Force for destroying their homes) featured prominently in the 'Epic Mickey' videogame?

1-10) In which city was Walt Disney born?

Answers to Question Set 1

1-1) Pete's Dragon was Elliott, voiced by Charlie Callas.

1-2) Donald Duck's middle name is Fauntleroy. He occasionally wears a Fauntleroy suit.

1-3) Keira Knightley played Elizabeth Swann, later to become Mrs Elizabeth Turner

1-4) Pluto's first appearance was in 'The Chain Gang' in 1930, though he wasn't given a name in that film. Later that year he appeared as Minnie's dog Rover in 'The Picnic. It wasn't until 1931's 'The Moose Hunt' that he became Mickey's pal Pluto.

1-5) The original build cost of Disneyland was $17 million.

1-6) In 'The Hunchback of Notre Dame' the voice of Esmeralda was provided by Demi Moore.

1-7) DisneySea was to have been built in the area of Long Beach around the Queen Mary ocean liner (which Disney also owned for a time).

1-8) Mickey Mouse's first film was 'Plane Crazy', but 'Steamboat Willie' and 'The Gallopin' Gaucho' – both made after 'Plane Crazy' – were both released before it. All three came out in 1928.

1-9) Work on 'The Gremlins' was halted in 1943. Gremlin Gus is Mickey's guide in the 'Epic Mickey' game.

1-10) Walt Disney was born in a suburb of Chicago, Illinois. His family later moved to Marceline, Missouri.

Question Set 2

2-1) What was the first ship in Disney's cruise line fleet?

2-2) Who voiced the Genie in the 'Aladdin' TV series?

2-3) What is the exclusive club and restaurant at Disneyland called?

2-4) In 'The Princess and the Frog', who provided the voice of Tiana's mother?

2-5) Name the two villainous cats in 'Lady and the Tramp'?

2-6) Who were Gruffi, Zummi, Cubbi, Sunni, Tummi and Grammi?

2-7) Which veteran horror actor recorded the narration for the Phantom Manor attraction at Disneyland Paris?

2-8) The name of which Disney animation Princess means 'Playful' in her native language?

2-9) What are employees of the Walt Disney Company know as?

2-10) What was the name of Walt Disney's wife?

Answers to Question Set 2

2-1) Disney Cruise Line's first ship was the Disney Magic.

2-2) Dan Castellaneta (best known as Homer Simpson's voice) provided the voice of the Genie in the 'Aladdin' TV series and the second of Disney's Aladdin films. He also recorded the soundtrack for 'Aladdin and the King of Thieves' before Robin Williams agreed to reprise his role as the Genie and rerecorded the whole lot.

2-3) Disneyland's private club and restaurant is Club 33. The waiting list for new membership is reported to be around 15 years. Tokyo Disneyland also has its own Club 33.

2-4) Oprah Winfrey plays Eudora, Tiana's mother in 'The Princess and the Frog'.

2-5) The evil Siamese cats from Lady and the Tramp are called Si and Am. Early in development they were to be called Nip and Tuck.

2-6) Gruffi, Zummi, Cubbi, Sunni, Tummi and Grammi were the six stars of 'Disney's Gummi Bears', the company's first animated TV series. It ran from 1985 to 1990.

2-7) Vincent Price was the Ghost Host when Phantom Manor – their version of the Haunted Mansion – opened at Disneyland Paris.

2-8) Pocahontas means 'Playful' in the Algonquin language.

2-9) Within the company, all Disney employees are referred to as 'cast members'.

2-10) Walt married Lillian Bounds in 1925.

Question Set 3

3-1) Which Disney movie inspired Steven Spielberg to make E.T.?

3-2) What is the name of Bambi's skunk friend?

3-3) Which two Walt Disney World minor theme parks are no longer open to the public?

3-4) What kind of fish is Nemo?

3-5) Who played 'Bert' in Mary Poppins?

3-6) Which Disney character sings 'Trust in Me'?

3-7) Where in Walt Disney World can you eat a Kitchen Sink?

3-8) How did Walt Disney do his patriotic duty in World War I?

3-9) What does the acronym EPCOT stand for?

3-10) What was the sequel to 'The Rescuers' called?

Answers to Question Set 3

3-1) Spielberg claimed that seeing 'Pete's Dragon' inspired him to create E.T.

3-2) Bambi's skunk friend is Flower.

3-3) River Country closed in 2001 and Discovery Island in 1999. A section of Disney's Animal Kingdom has now taken the 'Discovery Island' name.

3-4) Nemo is a clown fish.

3-5) Dick Van Dyke played Mary Poppins' friend Bert.

3-6) Sterling Holloway sang 'Trust in Me' as Kaa the python in 'The Jungle Book'.

3-7) A Kitchen Sink is a huge dessert (with everything thrown in it!) at the Beach Club's Beaches and Cream soda shop.

3-8) During the latter part of World War I, Walt Disney drove an ambulance in France for the Red Cross. He had wanted to join the army but was underage.

3-9) EPCOT was to be Walt Disney's Experimental Prototype Community Of Tomorrow. Sadly the park we see today bears little resemblance to Walt's dream.

3-10) 'The Rescuers' was followed by 'The Rescuers Down Under'.

Question Set 4

4-1) On what date did Walt Disney World open to the public?

4-2) Which Disney animated TV series featured many actors from the Star Trek franchise in its voice cast?

4-3) What did Emperor Hirohito of Japan wear all the time after being presented with it at Disneyland in 1978?

4-4) What number is painted on Herbie, the Love Bug?

4-5) What are the names of the three geese in 'The Aristocats'?

4-6) According to his television show's theme song, who was 'born on a mountain top in Tennessee'?

4-7) Which classic Disney animation featured Billy Joel and Bette Midler as the voices of two dogs?

4-8) What was the sequel to 'Fantasia' called?

4-9) Where in Walt Disney World can you watch sports on over one hundred TVs?

4-10) Who were Baldy, Puffy, Shorty, Lazy, Flabby, Deafy and Swift?

Answers to Question Set 4

4-1) Walt Disney World opened on October 1st 1971.

4-2) Many actors from the Star Trek TV and movie series provided the voices for Disney's 'Gargoyles' TV show.

4-3) Emperor Hirohito never went anywhere without his Mickey Mouse watch.

4-4) Herbie the Volkswagen Beetle sported the number 53.

4-5) The geese in 'The Aristocats' were the twins Abigail and Amelia Gabble and their drunken Uncle Waldo.

4-6) Davy Crockett was 'born on a mountain top in Tennessee'.

4-7) Billy Joel and Bette Midler provided voices for the 1988 release, 'Oliver and Company'.

4-8) 'Fantasia' was followed by 'Fantasia 2000'.

4-9) The ESPN Club at Disney's Boardwalk claims to have over a hundred television sets.

4-10) Baldy, Puffy, Shorty, Lazy, Flabby, Deafy and Swift were just seven of many suggested (but thankfully rejected) names for Snow White's Dwarfs.

Question Set 5

5-1) What lives beneath Sleeping Beauty's castle at Disneyland Paris?

5-2) Which famous artist worked with Disney on a short film called 'Destino'?

5-3) For which Disney animated classic did Michael J. Fox provide the voice of Milo Thatch?

5-4) In 'The Little Mermaid', what was the name of the sea witch?

5-5) And what was the name of her evil sister, seen in 'The Little Mermaid II: Return to the Sea'?

5-6) What terrifying apparition chases Ichabod Crane in 'The Adventures of Ichabod and Mr Toad'?

5-7) In 'The Aristocats', what are the names of Duchess's three kittens?

5-8) How many ghosts live in the Haunted Mansion?

5-9) Name the platypus in 'Phineas and Ferb'.

5-10) As what is Experiment 626 better known?

Answers to Question Set 5

5-1) Maleficent, a huge audio-animatronic dragon, is chained in the caverns deep beneath the castle at Disneyland Paris.

5-2) Salvador Dali and Walt Disney worked together on 'Destino' in 1945. The movie was shelved until Walt's nephew, Roy E. Disney, had it completed and released in 2003.

5-3) Michael J. Fox was the lead voice in 'Atlantis: The Lost Empire'.

5-4) The villainous sea witch in 'The Little Mermaid' was called Ursula.

5-5) Ursula's sister, Morgana, appeared in the sequel.

5-6) Ichabod Crane is chased by the Headless Horseman.

5-7) Duchess' Aristo-kittens are Marie, Toulouse and Berlioz.

5-8) There are 999 ghosts in the Haunted Mansion, but the ghost host says that there's always room for one more.

5-9) Phineas and Ferb's pet platypus is called Perry, but he is also known as Agent P.

5-10) Experiment 626 is more commonly known as Stitch.

Question Set 6

6-1) What kind of bird does Uncle Remus have on his shoulder?

6-2) What are the names of the children that Mary Poppins looks after?

6-3) In the Chip 'n Dale Rescue Rangers TV series, which character is named after a cheese?

6-4) In which other theme park is there a copy of Walt Disney World's Cinderella Castle?

6-5) In 'Enchanted', what is the name of the Prince?

6-6) On which attraction at EPCOT do riders reach speeds of up to 65 miles per hour?

6-7) Most cruise ships' horns just blare out a single note. What do the Disney Cruise Line ships' horns do?

6-8) Which American television company used to have a one third stake in Disneyland?

6-9) Which Disney live action movie was about a balloon crossing from East to West Germany?

6-10) What is the name of the purple dragon in EPCOT's Journey into Imagination ride?

Answers to Question Set 6

6-1) As he sings in Zip-A-Dee-Doo-Dah in 'Song of the South', Uncle Remus has a bluebird on his shoulder.

6-2) Mary Poppins is the nanny to Jane and Michael Banks.

6-3) Monterey Jack (or Monty) is the cheesy name of one of Chip 'n Dale's Rescue Rangers.

6-4) Tokyo Disneyland's castle is very similar to the one in Walt Disney World's Magic Kingdom.

6-5) Prince Edward comes to rescue Giselle in 'Enchanted'.

6-6) Reaching speeds of up to 65 mph, EPCOT's Test Track is Disney's fastest ride.

6-7) The horns on the Disney Cruise Line ships play 'When You Wish Upon A Star'... very loudly!

6-8) ABC had a one third shareholding in the Disneyland park.

6-9) The 1982 movie 'Night Crossing' showed a daring balloon flight to the freedom of West Germany.

6-10) Disney's purple dragon is called Figment.

Question Set 7

7-1) Who single-handedly drew every frame of the early Mickey Mouse cartoons?

7-2) What was Disney's first movie to be released under the Touchstone Pictures banner?

7-3) What are the ride vehicles called at the Haunted Mansion?

7-4) What was Walt Disney's full name?

7-5) Where in Walt Disney World can you ride the Grand 1 (if you're rich enough)?

7-6) Who were 'The Three Caballeros'?

7-7) What unusual action did Disney animators take on May 29 1941?

7-8) In which live action movie did Madonna star as Breathless Mahoney?

7-9) What was the name of Mickey Mouse's wizard teacher in 'The Sorcerer's Apprentice'?

7-10) ...and who was the sorcerer played by Nicholas Cage in the live action version?

Answers to Question Set 7

7-1) Disney legend Ub Iwerks animated most of Mickey's early movies.

7-2) 'Splash', starring Tom Hanks and Daryl Hannah, was the first Touchstone movie.

7-3) Haunted Mansion riders sit in a 'Doom Buggy'.

7-4) Walter Elias Disney was named for his father (Elias Disney) and his parents' good friend and local preacher, Reverend Walter Parr. The Reverend Parr would later name his own new-born son Walter Elias Parr.

7-5) The Grand 1 is a 52-foot motor yacht available for hire on the Seven Seas Lagoon and Bay Lake at Walt Disney World. It's big enough for 17 guests plus captain, deck hand and butler.

7-6) Donald Duck, Panchito Pistoles and Jose Carioca were 'The Three Caballeros'.

7-7) On May 29 1941Disney animators began a bitter strike which lasted five weeks.

7-8) Madonna played Breathless in 'Dick Tracy'.

7-9) The original Sorcerer was called Yen Sid, which is Disney backwards.

7-10) In the live action 'Sorcerer's Apprentice' movie Nicolas Cage plays Balthazar Blake.

Question Set 8

8-1) On which Disney ride can you hear the cry, 'We wants the redhead'?

8-2) Which Disney characters are known in France as Tic et Tac?

8-3) What is the name of the cat in 'Cinderella'?

8-4) Which Gary K. Wolfe novel was filmed as 'Who Framed Roger Rabbit?'

8-5) Which very early Disney series featured a live action girl interacting with animated characters and backgrounds?

8-6) Who is the only title character in a classic Disney animation feature movie that doesn't speak?

8-7) Which voice part does Jeremy Irons play in 'The Lion King'?

8-8) Why is Walt Disney World's Tower of Terror ride 'just' 199 feet high?

8-9) There's only one ride at Walt Disney World that is higher than the Tower of Terror. Name it.

8-10) What was the name of 2001 movie spin-off from the 'Recess' TV series?

Answers to Question Set 8

8-1) One of the most famous lines on any Disney attraction is 'We wants the redhead!' on Pirates of the Caribbean.

8-2) Tic et Tac are the French names for Chip and Dale.

8-3) The evil cat in 'Cinderella' is Lucifer.

8-4) Gary K. Wolfe's original novel was called 'Who Censored Roger Rabbit?'

8-5) The 'Alice Comedies' featured a young girl in a cartoon world.

8-6) Dumbo doesn't speak in his original movie, although he was given a voice in TV series, 'Dumbo's Circus'.

8-7) In 'The Lion King' Jeremy Irons voices the evil uncle Scar.

8-8) The Tower of Terror is 199 feet tall. The Federal Aviation Administration requires that all buildings over 200 feet have a fixed red beacon on top.

8-9) Expedition Everest is Walt Disney World's tallest ride at 199 feet and six inches.

8-10) The 'Recess' TV series made the jump to movies with 'Recess: School's Out' in 2001.

Question Set 9

9-1) What was the name of the town built on Walt Disney World property in 1996?

9-2) In 'The Emperor's New Groove', into what kind of animal is Kuzco turned?

9-3) Walt Disney's son-in-law, Ron W. Miller, played which sport professionally?

9-4) Who were the American television hosts for 'The Grand Opening of Euro Disney'?

9-5) Who is Nemo's dad?

9-6) A replica of which famous ship sails at Disneyland?

9-7) Which cartoon series featured versions of many 'Jungle Book' characters?

9-8) What was the last full length animation in which Walt Disney was personally involved?

9-9) What are the tunnels beneath Walt Disney World's Magic Kingdom called?

9-10) Who was officially crowned as Disney's 10th Princess?

Answers to Question Set 9

9-1) The town of 20,000 residents near to Walt Disney World is called Celebration.

9-2) Kuzco becomes a llama in 'The Emperor's New Groove'.

9-3) Ron W. Miller was the quarterback for the Los Angeles Rams NFL team and married Walt's daughter, Diane. He later became President and CEO of Walt Disney Productions.

9-4) The Grand Opening of Euro Disney's American TV hosts were Melanie Griffiths and Don Johnson. Each country to broadcast the event had their own local TV hosts.

9-5) Nemo's father is called Marlin.

9-6) Passengers can ride on the Sailing Ship Columbia at Disneyland, a replica of the first American ship to sail around the world.

9-7) 'TaleSpin' starred Balloo, Shere Khan and King Louie from the Jungle Book

9-8) 'The Jungle Book' was the last full length animation on which Walt personally worked.

9-9) Beneath the Magic Kingdom are a series of Utilidors via which staff can travel without being seen by the public.

9-10) Rapunzel became Disney's 10th Princess at a coronation ceremony at London's Kensington Palace on 2nd of October 2011.

Question Set 10

10-1) Who was the single biggest shareholder in the Walt Disney Company at the time of his death in 2011?

10-2) In which Disney movie did Susan Sarandon play the part of the evil queen?

10-3) Which 1957 Disney live action film about a stray dog has one of the saddest endings in movie history?

10-4) What is the name of the restaurant in EPCOT's Canada pavilion, famous for its cheddar cheese soup?

10-5) ... and on which Ottawa landmark is the building which houses the restaurant modelled?

10-6) Don Rosa and Carl Barks are primarily known for working on what?

10-7) What were the group of long-serving artists who worked with Walt Disney informally known as?

10-8) At which Disneyland Paris dinner show would you receive a free cowboy hat?

10-9) Which animated character from 'Pinocchio' went on to appear in seven short films of their own?

10-10) Which miniature golf course at Walt Disney World is themed around a classic Disney animation?

Answers to Question Set 10

10-1) Steve Jobs was Disney's biggest single individual shareholder.

10-2) Susan Sarandon was the villainous Queen Narissa in 'Enchanted'.

10-3) At the end of 'Old Yeller', the dog contracts rabies and has to be shot.

10-4) EPCOT's Canadian restaurant is called Le Cellier.

10-5) ...and from the outside it looks like the Fairmont Chateau Laurier.

10-6) Don Rosa and Carl Barks are best known for their work on Donald and Scrooge McDuck comic books.

10-7) Walt's closest artists were referred to as The Nine Old Men.

10-8) Everyone at Buffalo Bill's Wild West Show receives a free cowboy hat.

10-9) Figaro the cute kitten from 'Pinocchio' later starred in a series of shorts.

10-10) Walt Disney World's Fantasia Gardens mini golf is based around scenes from 'Fantasia'.

Question Set 11

11-1) Walt Disney's final press conference was to talk about which ski resort?

11-2) In 'The Sword In The Stone', the boy who would grow up to be King Arthur is called what?

11-3) Which creepy 1981 live action Disney movie starred an aging Bette Davis as Mrs Alywood?

11-4) What do Gill and the other fish in the dentist's office call Nemo?

11-5) At Disneyland, what was above the fire station on Main Street?

11-6) What is the name of Ariel's daughter?

11-7) What is the name of the famous statue of Walt and Mickey Mouse in the Magic Kingdom?

11-8) What is the name of the evil one-eyed grasshopper in 'A Bug's Life'?

11-9) Which Disney heroine has friends called Mushu and Cri-Kee?

11-10) At whose party might you eat unbirthday cake?

Answers to Question Set 11

11-1) Disney's proposed ski resort was to be at Mineral King in the Sierra Nevada Mountains, California.

11-2) Young Arthur is referred to as 'Wart' throughout 'The Sword in the Stone'.

11-3) Bette Davis starred as Mrs Alywood in 'The Watcher in the Woods'.

11-4) The other fish call Nemo 'Sharkbait'.

11-5) Walt Disney built his private apartment above Disneyland's fire house.

11-6) The Little Mermaid's daughter is called Melody.

11-7) Hal Blaine's magnificent statue of Walt and Mickey is simply called 'Partners'.

11-8) The villain in 'A Bug's Life' is called Hopper.

11-9) Mushu and Cri-Kee are friends of Mulan.

11-10) Unbirthday cake is served at the Mad Hatter's tea party.

Question Set 12

12-1) To which magical island does Angela Lansbury take three children (on a travelling bed) in 'Bedknobs and Broomsticks'?

12-2) Apart from pink elephants, of which animals did Pooh Bear dream?

12-3) What opened at Walt Disney World to celebrate Mickey's 60th birthday?

12-4) At EPCOT, for what have Vic Perrin, Walter Kronkite, Jeremy Irons and Dame Judi Dench all been responsible?

12-5) On which actress was Tinker Bell's physical appearance based?

12-6) In the Lion King, who is Simba's girlfriend?

12-7) Where was the Carolwood Pacific Railroad?

12-8) What are the Banana Blaster, Coconut Crusher and Pineapple Plunger?

12-9) Who is 'Practically Perfect in Every Way'?

12-10) In 'Hercules', who voiced the evil Hades?

Answers to Question Set 12

12-1) In 'Bedknobs and Broomsticks' the bed travels to the Isle of Naboombu.

12-2) Winnie the Pooh dreams of Heffalumps and Woozles.

12-3) Mickey's Birthdayland opened in 1988. It was later renamed Mickey's Starland and later still Mickey's Toontown Fair before closing in 2011.

12-4) Vic Perrin, Walter Kronkite, Jeremy Irons and Dame Judi Dench have all provided narration for Spaceship Earth.

12-5) Artist Marc Davis based Tinker Bell's figure on that of actress Margaret Kerry and not, as urban legend commonly has it, Marilyn Monroe.

12-6) Simba's girlfriend was Nala.

12-7) The Carolwood Pacific Railroad was Walt Disney's private $1/8^{th}$ scale railway set up in the garden of his home.

12-8) They are the three slides of Typhoon Lagoon's Crush 'n' Gusher.

12-9) Mary Poppins is 'Practically Perfect in Every Way'.

12-10) James Woods was the voice of Hades.

Question Set 13

13-1) What was Hayley Mills' last big screen movie for Disney? Released in 1965, it was based on Mildred and Gordon Gordon's novel, 'Undercover Cat'.

13-2) Which piece of music by Prokofiev was turned into animation by Disney, just as the composer had hoped?

13-3) In 'Finding Nemo', which character is voiced by Ellen DeGeneres?

13-4) Which of Disneyland Paris Resort's hotels has a Wild West theme?

13-5) Which Disney couple famously shared a dish of spaghetti and meatballs at Tony's Italian restaurant?

13-6) When it originally opened at Disney's Animal Kingdom Park, what was the ride we now know as Dinosaur called?

13-7) 'Suite Life on Deck' is the sequel to which Disney Channel series?

13-8) In Walt Disney World, where would you find Sonny Eclipse and the Space Angels?

13-9) Which animals made an 'Incredible Journey' in the 1963 movie?

13-10) ...and who provided the main three voices for the 1993 'Homeward Bound' remake?

Answers to Question Set 13

13-1) Hayley Mills' final film for Disney was 'That Darn Cat'.

13-2) Sergei Prokofiev wrote 'Peter and the Wolf' in 1936. Disney made an animated version of the story ten years later.

13-3) Ellen DeGeneres was the voice of Dory.

13-4) The cowboy-themed hotel at Disneyland Paris is the Hotel Cheyenne.

13-5) Lady and (the) Tramp ate at Tony's.

13-6) The Dinosaur ride was originally called Countdown To Extinction, but was renamed to tie in with the 'Dinosaur' movie.

13-7) 'Suite Life on Deck' followed 'The Suite Life of Zack and Cody.

13-8) Sonny Eclipse, along with his invisible backing group The Space Angels, sings at the Starlight Lounge Room of Cosmic Ray's Starlight Cafe in Tomorrowland.

13-9) The animals in the original 'Incredible Journey' movie were a Labrador, a Bull Terrier and a Siamese cat.

13-10) Don Ameche, Michael J Fox and Sally Field voiced the animals in 'Homeward Bound: The Incredible Journey'. Fox and Field returned, but Ralph Waite replaced the deceased Ameche in the sequel, 'Homeward Bound II: Lost in San Francisco'.

Question Set 14

14-1) Name 'The Fox and the Hound'.

14-2) For what event did Disney create Great Moments with Mr Lincoln, It's a Small World, the Magic Skyway and the Carousel of Progress?

14-3) The story of 'The Lion King' loosely follows that of which Shakespeare play?

14-4) What was the name of the American history-based theme park that Disney had planned in the mid 'nineties?

14-5) The third and final direct-to-video movie based on 'Lilo and Stitch' was called who 'and Stitch'?

14-6) Which loveable rogues have trouble coexisting with Donald Duck in 'Out of Scale', 'Winter Storage' and 'Out on a Limb'?

14-7) For which animated film was the song Music In Your Soup written and roughly drawn but ultimately cut?

14-8) Where in Walt Disney World is there a huge disused wave machine?

14-9) There is a famous statue (called 'Partners') of Walt Disney holding hands with Mickey Mouse. But who features in a similar statue sitting on a bench with Minnie?

14-10) In 'Enchanted', where does Giselle come from?

Answers to Question Set 14

14-1) The names of 'The Fox and the Hound' were Tod and Copper.

14-2) Great Moments with Mr Lincoln, It's a Small World, the Magic Skyway and the Carousel of Progress were all created for the 1964 World's Fair in New York.

14-3) 'The Lion King's plot is broadly similar to that of 'Hamlet'.

14-4) Disney's America would have been a history themed park in Virginia.

14-5) The final Stitch adventure was called 'Leroy and Stitch'.

14-6) Donald Duck was constantly at war with Chip an' Dale.

14-7) Music in Your Soup was recorded and drawn but withdrawn from 'Snow White and the Seven Dwarfs'.

14-8) Bay Lake has a sunken machine to create waves big enough to surf on at the Polynesian Resort beach. Unfortunately it would have created serious erosion at the beach and so was never put in regular service.

14-9) Sculptor Blaine Gibson created 'Partners' (featuring Mickey and Walt) and 'Sharing the Magic' which shows Minnie seated on a park bench alongside Walt's brother, Roy O. Disney.

14-10) 'Enchanted's Giselle comes from Andalasia.

Question Set 15

15-1) In 'Beauty and the Beast', what is the name of Belle's horse?

15-2) Who wrote the original book 'The Hundred and One Dalmatians'?

15-3) What does 'Hakuna Matata' really mean?

15-4) John Rzeznik of The Goo Goo Dolls wrote songs for which Disney animation?

15-5) Where will Mystic Point be when it opens (as scheduled) in 2013?

15-6) Which brothers wrote 'The Wonderful Thing about Tiggers', 'It's a Small World (after all)', 'The Bare Necessities' and many other classic Disney songs?

15-7) Disney claims that each of their cruise ships has four captains. One is the human responsible for the ship, but who are the other three?

15-8) What beloved Disneyland attraction's distinctive theme tune is called 'Baroque Hoedown'?

15-9) What is Aladdin's monkey friend called?

15-10) Where can you walk through the Nautilus submarine from '20,000 Leagues Under the Sea' and witness the ship being attacked by a giant squid?

Answers to Question Set 15

15-1) Belle's horse is called Phillipe.

15-2) Dodie Smith published 'The Hundred and One Dalmatians' in 1956. She wrote a sequel – 'The Starlight Barking' – nine years later.

15-3) 'Hakuna Matata' literally means 'there are no problems' in Swahili.

15-4) John Rzeznik wrote songs for 'Treasure Planet'.

15-5) Mystic Point is a new land which is scheduled to open at Hong Kong Disneyland in 2013.

15-6) Robert and Richard Sherman were staff songwriters for Walt Disney productions.

15-7) On each Disney cruise, as well as the human Captain, you may see Captain Hook, Captain Jack Sparrow and Captain Mickey Mouse.

15-8) 'Baroque Hoedown' is the theme tune for the Main Street Electrical Parade.

15-9) Aladdin's monkey is Abu.

15-10) Guests can walk through Captain Nemo's submarine at Les Mystères du Nautilus attraction (The Mysteries of the Nautilus) at Disneyland Paris.

Question Set 16

16-1) Which British drummer wrote songs for 'Tarzan' and 'Brother Bear'?

16-2) What colour are Figment the dragons' wings?

16-3) In 'The Princess Diaries', what country does Mia end up ruling?

16-4) Which group feature heavily on the Rock 'n' Roller Coaster attraction?

16-5) ...but which, arguably more famous, rock band were approached to front the ride at first?

16-6) Who wrote songs for 'The Lion King'?

16-7) Which 1965 live action movie starred a Siamese called Syn?

16-8) In which wood does Pooh Bear live?

16-9) Whose official address is Hangman's Tree, Never Land, Second Star to the Right?

16-10) Who is the girlfriend of Ron Stoppable?

Answers to Question Set 16

16-1) Phil Collins wrote the songs for 'Tarzan' and 'Brother Bear'.

16-2) Figment's wings are orange.

16-3) 'The Princess Diaries' are about the Princess of Genovia.

16-4) Aerosmith are the business and musical face of the Rock 'n' Roller Coaster.

16-5) ...but the Rolling Stones had been approached first. Their financial demands were allegedly more than Disney was willing to pay.

16-6) Elton John wrote songs for 'The Lion King'.

16-7) Syn was the star of 'That Darn Cat'.

16-8) Pooh lives in the Hundred-Acre Wood.

16-9) Tinker Bell lives at Hangman's tree.

16-10) Ron Stoppable's girlfriend is Kim Possible.

Question Set 17

17-1) Who wrote songs for 'Robin Hood'?

17-2) Which Disney character starred in a series of shorts in the 1940's and 1950's called 'How To...'?

17-3) The artist Gerald Scarfe famously designed the villains for which Disney feature?

17-4) The rock star Mega Dork sports a Mickey Mouse tattoo in which movie?

17-5) Who is known as Paperino in Italy?

17-6) 'Bear Country', 'The African Lion' and 'Beaver Valley' were all in which series of live action films?

17-7) Bob Newhart and Eva Gabor voiced the main characters in which Disney classic, as well as its sequel?

17-8) Who were the Firehouse Five Plus Two?

17-9) What are Mickey Mouse's nephews called?

17-10) Where will a new Disneyland open in 2016?

Answers to Question Set 17

17-1) Roger Miller (who had a hit with 'King of the Road') wrote songs for ''Robin Hood'.

17-2) Goofy starred in the 'How To...' series.

17-3) Gerald Scarfe designed characters for 'Hercules'.

17-4) Mega Dork and his tattoo appear in 'Toy Story' – on a poster in Sid's room.

17-5) The Italians call Donald Duck 'Paperino'.

17-6) 'Bear Country', 'The African Lion' and 'Beaver Valley' were all True-Life Adventure films.

17-7) Bob Newhart and Eva Gabor were the voices of Bernard and Bianca in 'The Rescuers' and 'The Rescuers Down Under'.

17-8) The Firehouse Five Plus Two were a jazz group made up of Disney filmmakers. They recorded several albums in the 1940s and '50s.

17-9) Mickey's nephews are called Morty and Ferdie Fieldmouse.

17-10) Shanghai Disneyland is scheduled to open in China in 2016.

Question Set 18

18-1) What kind of plaything is 'Toy Story's 'Ham'?

18-2) What creature plays with a yo-yo in 'Fantasia 2000'?

18-3) Which live action Disney movie starred Sean Connery and a cast of leprechauns?

18-4) At EPCOT's old The Living Seas pavilion, where would 'hydrolators' take visitors?

18-5) What classic Disney song did Gene Simmons of the rock group Kiss record for his first solo album?

18-6) Which conductor shakes hands with Mickey Mouse in 'Fantasia'?

18-7) What was the first Disney animated movie to be adapted as a Broadway show?

18-8) Which Disney character's first names are Horatio Felonious Ignacious Crustaceous...?

18-9) First running in 1991, what is the popular night-time parade at Walt Disney World's Magic Kingdom called?

18-10) Which early Disney character was the star of 'Sagebush Sadie', 'Ride 'em, Plow Boy' and 'The Ocean Hop'?

Answers to Question Set 18

18-1) Ham is a piggy bank.

18-2) A flamingo plays with a yo-yo in 'Fantasia 2000'. The music used is The Carnival of the Animals by Camille Saint-Saens.

18-3) Sean Connery was in 'Darby O'Gill and the Little People'.

18-4) The Living Seas' 'hydrolators' used to descend to Sea Base Alpha.

18-5) Gene Simmons sang a version of 'When You Wish Upon a Star' which was very true to the original.

18-6) Leopold Stokowski appears with Mickey in Fantasia.

18-7) 'Snow White and the Seven Dwarfs' opened on Broadway in 1979.

18-8) Ariel's crab friend's full name is Horatio Felonious Ignacious Crustaceous Sebastian.

18-9) Walt Disney World's night-time parade is called Spectromagic.

18-10) The star of 'Sagebush Sadie', Ride 'em plow Boy' and 'The Ocean Hop' was Oswald the Lucky Rabbit.

Question Set 19

19-1) What kind of animal did Pinocchio begin to turn into when he behaved badly?

19-2) What was the name of the animated version of 'My Fair Lady' that Disney had planned? It would have had an elephant as the lead, but was eventually cancelled in 2000.

19-3) In which Disney channel movie series did Debbie Reynolds play the role of Aggie Cromwell?

19-4) In which short film did Goofy say 'I ain't scared of no ghosts'?

19-5) What word was removed from the original name of Disney's Animal Kingdom?

19-6) The deep voice behind Tony the Tiger ("They're grrreeeat!") also sang lead vocal on which much-loved Disney ride theme song?

19-7) What is the name of Pocahontas' grandma?

19-8) What would the Californian version of EPCOT have been called, had it come to fruition?

19-9) Cornelius Coot was the founder of which town?

19-10) In 'Lion King II: Simba's Pride', what is the name of Simba and Nala's daughter?

Answers to Question Set 19

19-1) Pinocchio began to turn into a donkey, because he was behaving like an ass.

19-2) 'Wild Life' was cancelled in 2000 due to its adult themes and jokes.

19-3) Debbie Reynolds played Aggie Cromwell in 'Halloweentown' and its sequels.

19-4) Mickey, Donald and Goofy worked as ghost busters in 'Lonesome Ghosts'.

19-5) Disney's Animal Kingdom was originally to have been called Disney's WILD Animal Kingdom.

19-6) Thurl Ravenscroft was both Tony the Tiger and the lead singer on 'Grim Grinning Ghosts'.

19-7) Pocahontas' granny is called Grandmother Willow. She's a tree.

19-8) The planned Californian version of EPCOT was to have been called WestCOT.

19-9) Cornelius Coot was the founder of Duckburg, Donald's hometown.

19-10) Simba and Nala's daughter is Kiara.

Question Set 20

20-1) Disney's 'Robin Hood' was an animation, but what was the company's 1952 live action version of the story called?

20-2) The Cheetah Girls and Belinda Carlisle have both recorded covers of which song from the movie 'Hercules'?

20-3) In which animated short film did Donald Duck learn the importance of numbers?

20-4) What is 'the wildest ride in the wilderness'?

20-5) Which land in Disney's California Adventure is its version of Main Street USA?

20-6) How old was Walt Disney when he died?

20-7) Which Disney TV series was a spin-off from 'The Emperor's New Groove'?

20-8) What is Donald Duck's penny-pinching uncle called?

20-9) Who was the male star of the movie 'The Haunted Mansion'?

20-10) ...and who was the male star of the TV movie 'The Tower of Terror'?

Answers to Question Set 20

20-1) Disney's live action Robin Hood movie was 'The Story of Robin Hood and His Merrie Men'.

20-2) The Cheetah Girls and Belinda Carlisle have both covered 'I Won't Say (I'm in Love)'.

20-3) Donald learned all about numbers in 'Donald in Mathmagic Land'.

20-4) Announcements made to those waiting to ride Big Thunder Mountain Railroad claim it to be 'the wildest ride in the wilderness'.

20-5) Guests enter Disney's California Adventure through Buena Vista Street, formerly known as Sunshine Plaza.

20-6) Walt Disney died ten days after his 65th birthday.

20-7) 'The Emperor's New School' was the TV series based on 'The Emperor's New Groove'.

20-8) Donald's uncle is Scrooge McDuck.

20-9) Eddie Murphy starred in 'The Haunted Mansion'.

20-10) Steve Guttenberg starred in 'The Tower of Terror'.

Question Set 21

21-1) Belle, Pumbaa and Aladdin's flying carpet all make cameo appearances in which animated feature?

21-2) Which live action Disney movie featured bad guys the Nome King and Princess Mombi, and good guys Tik-Tok and Jack Pumpkinhead?

21-3) What was the first film in the 'Silly Symphony' series?

21-4) In 1999 what did Disneyland's Swiss Family Treehouse become?

21-5) Which Disney TV series featured supporting characters Maurice the gorilla, Stewart the elephant and Eduardo the jaguar?

21-6) What is the title of the animated short which shows Rapunzel marrying Flynn Rider?

21-7) How many Disney animated classics have won the Academy Award for Best Animated Feature (up to February 2012)?

21-8) How many Pixar movies have won the Academy Award for Best Animated Feature (up to February 2012)?

21-9) What was the last film in the 'Silly Symphony' series?

21-10) 'Disney After Dark', 'Disney at Dawn' and 'Disney in Shadow' are the first three books in which series?

Answers to Question Set 21

21-1) Belle, Pumbaa and Aladdin's flying carpet all appear in 'The Hunchback of Notre Dame'.

21-2) The Nome King, Princess Mombi, Tik-Tok and Jack Pumpkinhead were all in 'Return to Oz'.

21-3) The first film in the 'Silly Symphony' series was 'The Skeleton Dance' from 1929.

21-4) Swiss Family Treehouse was changed to Tarzan's Treehouse at Disneyland.

21-5) Maurice the gorilla, Stewart the elephant and Eduardo the jaguar all appeared in 'Marsupilami'.

21-6) 'Tangled Ever After' was the six minute sequel to 'Tangled'.

21-7) At the time of writing, no Disney classic animation has ever won the Best Animated Feature Oscar since it was introduced in 2001.

21-8) At the time of writing, Pixar have won the Best Animated Feature Oscar on six occasions – 'Finding Nemo', 'The Incredibles', 'Ratatouille', 'WALL-E', 'Up!' and 'Toy Story 3'.

21-9) The final film in the 'Silly Symphony' series was 'The Ugly Duckling' from 1939. This was a remake of a 1931 version of the film.

21-10) 'Disney After Dark', 'Disney at Dawn' and 'Disney in Shadow' are the first three books in the Kingdom Keepers series.

Question Set 22

22-1) Which pavilion in EPCOT contains Soarin', and the Garden Grill restaurant?

22-2) Youngsters Britney Spears, Christina Aguilera and Justin Timberlake all regularly appeared in which Disney Channel TV show in 1993 and '94?

22-3) What is Goofy's son called?

22-4) What 3D movie that performed at EPCOT from 1986 starred Michael Jackson?

22-5) What was Disney's first full length movie to not feature any animation at all?

22-6) What is The Electric Umbrella?

22-7) The Walt Disney Company were the first owners of which NHL ice hockey team?

22-8) Which Disney TV character's catchphrase was 'Let's get dangerous!'?

22-9) What was Walt's 'top secret' name for Walt Disney World?

22-10) What are Donald Duck's triplet nieces called?

Answers to Question Set 22

22-1) Soarin', and the Garden Grill restaurant are in The Land pavilion at EPCOT.

22-2) Britney, Christina and Justin all appeared on the Mickey Mouse Club.

22-3) Goofy's son is called Max Goof.

22-4) Michael Jackson starred in 'Captain EO'.

22-5) Disney's first completely live action movie was 'Treasure Island' in 1950.

22-6) The Electric Umbrella is a quick service restaurant at EPCOT's Futureworld.

22-7) The Walt Disney Company founded the Mighty Ducks of Anaheim, now known as the Anaheim Ducks.

22-8) Darkwing Duck's battle cry was 'Let's get dangerous!'

22-9) Walt referred to (what would eventually become) Walt Disney World as 'Project X' and 'The Florida Project'.

22-10) Donald's nieces are April, May and June Duck.

Question Set 23

23-1) Who has appeared in more Disney movies than any other character?

23-2) What is the name of the paddle steamer moored at Walt Disney World's Pleasure Island?

23-3) Austrian novelist Felix Salten wrote which novel that later became a classic Disney animation?

23-4) What is the name of Mickey's dinner club theatre in the Disney Channel TV series that ran from 2001 to 2003?

23-5) Who is 'the mistress of all evil' in 'Sleeping Beauty'?

23-6) Why does Walt Disney have two stars on the Hollywood Walk of Fame?

23-7) Which theme park opened in 2001 as an expansion of Disneyland resort?

23-8) What series of live action films feature a golden retriever (who excels at various sports) and his puppies?

23-9) What was the film industry's disparaging nickname for 'Snow White and the Seven Dwarfs'?

23-10) The Walt Disney World trains spend the night in the lower section of a building called The Roundhouse. What is on the upper floor?

Answers to Question Set 23

23-1) Donald Duck is Disney's most prolific star.

23-2) Pleasure Island's paddle steamer is the Empress Lilly, named after Walt's wife, Lillian Disney.

23-3) Felix Salten wrote 'Bambi, A Life in the Woods'.

23-4) Mickey's dinner club theatre was 'The House of Mouse'.

23-5) 'Sleeping Beauty's villain is Maleficent.

23-6) One of Walt Disney's stars on the Hollywood Walk of Fame is in recognition of his movies; the other is for his television work.

23-7) Disneyland Resort's second theme park is Disney's California Adventure.

23-8) Buddy and his puppies are the stars of the 'Air Bud' film series.

23-9) Before its release 'Snow White' was referred to in the industry as 'Disney's Folly'.

23-10) The Walt Disney World monorails spend the night in the upper section of The Roundhouse, above the trains.

Question Set 24

24-1) What is the name of the 12,000 acre natural conservation area approximately 12 miles south of Walt Disney World?

24-2) Which 1985 Disney animated movie was based on Lloyd Alexander's 'Chronicles of Prydain' series of books?

24-3) Opened in 1987, where was the first ever Disney Store?

24-4) Which movie features the song, 'Colors of the Wind'.

24-5) At which theme park does the S.S.Columbia dominate the American Waterfront?

24-6) What is the name of Disney's private island in the Bahamas, where many of the Disney cruises call in?

24-7) What female chipmunk do Chip and Dale disagree over in 'Two Chips and a Miss'?

24-8) The name of which magical substance from 'The Absent-Minded Professor' (1961) was used as the title of that film's 1997 remake?

24-9) What is the name of the dog that the Darling family use as a nursemaid in 'Peter Pan'?

24-10) Comedian Lenny Henry played a black actor who (on the run from the Mafia) is disguised as a white man in which Touchstone comedy?

Answers to Question Set 24

24-1) Disney's Wilderness Preserve was America's first large-scale, off-site wetlands mitigation project and is open to the public.

24-2) 'The Black Cauldron' was based on 'The Chronicles of Prydain'.

24-3) The first Disney Store was in Glendale, California.

24-4) 'Colors of the Wind' was in 'Pocahontas'.

24-5) The S.S.Columbia and the American Waterfront are at Tokyo DisneySea.

24-6) Disney's private island in the Bahamas is Castaway Cay.

24-7) 'Two Chips and a Miss' stars Chip, Dale and a lady chipmunk called Clarice.

24-8) The remake of 'The Absent-Minded Professor' was 'Flubber'.

24-9) The dog in 'Peter Pan' was called Nana.

24-10) 'True Identity' (1991) was the first of a proposed three film deal between Disney and Lenny Henry.

Question Set 25

25-1) What is the extremely popular pineapple sorbet snack that is served at Walt Disney World parks?

25-2) Which musical film from 1992 featured newspaper sellers in New York City?

25-3) Which Disney TV series spawned a spin-off movie called 'Treasure of the Lost Lamp'?

25-4) What was the final Disney movie to use the traditional technique of hand-painted cells for almost the entire film?

25-5) What kind of creatures are Robin and Marion in the animated classic, 'Robin Hood'?

25-6) The castle at Disneyland takes its name from which Disney Princess?

25-7) The castle at Walt Disney takes its name from which Disney Princess?

25-8) Of which Disney park did respected long-time Imagineer John Hench reportedly say, 'I liked it better as a parking lot'?

25-9) What is the name of the mouse who is Dumbo's only friend?

25-10) Which Disney film features Penny and her dog (who thinks that he's a superhero)?

Answers to Question Set 25

25-1) The pineapple sorbet snack is called a Dole Whip.

25-2) 'Newsies' was a loosely based on a strike by newspaper sellers in 1899.

25-3) 'Treasure of the Lost Lamp' was also known as 'DuckTales: The Movie'.

25-4) The last traditionally animated Disney movie was 'The Little Mermaid' (1989).

25-5) Robin and Marion are foxes.

25-6) Disneyland, Hong Kong Disneyland and Disneyland Paris all have a Sleeping Beauty Castle although the French version looks very different to the others.

25-7) Walt Disney World and Tokyo Disneyland each have a Cinderella Castle.

25-8) John Hench was unimpressed by Disney's California Adventure.

25-9) Dumbo's friend is Timothy Q. Mouse.

25-10) 'Bolt' thinks he's a superhero.

Question Set 26

26-1) What is the current name of the tower block that has previously been known as the Pan Pacific hotel and the Disneyland Pacific hotel?

26-2) What was the space-age fiberglass dwelling built in Disneyland in 1957?

26-3) Which computer animated movie features Lewis, an orphaned young inventor?

26-4) Who played Blackbeard in 'Pirates of the Caribbean: On Stranger Tides'?

26-5) ...and who played Blackbeard in 'Blackbeard's Ghost'?

26-6) In 'The Lion King', what is the baboon called?

26-7) What does Lots-o'-Huggin' Bear smell of in 'Toy Story 3'?

26-8) Which work by Rudyard Kipling became a Disney animation classic?

26-9) In what country was Walt Disney's father, Elias, born?

26-10) What is Cinderella's evil stepmother called?

Answers to Question Set 26

26-1) The Pan Pacific hotel is now Disney's Paradise Pier hotel.

26-2) From 1957 to 1967 Disneyland visitors could walk through the Monsanto House of the Future.

26-3) Lewis is the star of 'Meet the Robinsons'.

26-4) Ian McShane played the part of the pirate Blackbeard in 2011.

26-5) ...while Peter Ustinov took on the same role in 1968.

26-6) 'The Lion King's baboon is Rafiki.

26-7) Lotso smells of strawberries.

26-8) Rudyard Kipling wrote 'The Jungle Book'.

26-9) Elias Disney was born in Ontario, Canada.

26-10) Cinderella's stepmother is the Lady Tremaine.

Question Set 27

27-1) Peg Leg Pete has been Mickey's nemesis since 'Steamboat Willie'. But in which film series did he first appear?

27-2) In which theme park ride are guests launched out of the Columbiad Cannon?

27-3) Which hugely successful video game series features Disney characters as well as stars of the Final Fantasy games?

27-4) Walt Disney came up with the idea for the Matterhorn Bobsleds ride while filming which movie in Switzerland?

27-5) Name the two main bears in 'Brother Bear'.

27-6) Which satyr trained 'Hercules'?

27-7) What is the white-knuckle raft ride at Disney California Adventure?

27-8) What is Flynn's horse called in 'Tangled'?

27-9) And what similar name does the killer robot have in 'The Black Hole'?

27-10) Which renowned NFL coach has a steakhouse in Walt Disney World's Dolphin hotel?

Answers to Question Set 27

27-1) Pete first appeared in the 'Alice Comedies'.

27-2) The Columbiad Cannon is the launch section of Space Mountain at Disneyland Paris.

27-3) Disney meets Final Fantasy in the 'Kingdom Hearts' series of games.

27-4) Walt was in Switzerland filming 'Third Man on the Mountain'.

27-5) 'Brother Bear' stars Kenai and Koda.

27-6) Hercules's trainer was Philoctetes, though he lets Hercules call him Phil.

27-7) Grizzly River Run at Disney California Adventure is the longest, tallest, fastest white-water rapids ride ever built.

27-8) Flynn's horse is Maximus...

27-9) ...whereas 'The Black Hole's killer robot was Maximilian.

27-10) Don Shula of the Miami Dolphins owns Shula's Steakhouse at the Walt Disney World Dolphin hotel.

Question Set 28

28-1) What is the lake called that separates Walt Disney World's Ticket and Transportation Center from the Magic Kingdom? Guests travel over it either by boat or monorail.

28-2) Which Disney princess is known by three distinctly separate names?

28-3) What was Daisy Duck called on her first film appearance, in 1937's 'Don Donald'?

28-4) Which barber shop quartet perform regularly at Disneyland and the Magic Kingdom?

28-5) Where is Toy Story Land?

28-6) What are the two main comedic mice called in 'Cinderella'?

28-7) Mannequins, 8TRAX and the Neon Armadillo were all where?

28-8) Which Danish theme park did Walt use as a basic template for Disneyland?

28-9) What is the title of the prequel to 'Monsters, Inc.'?

28-10) Who, according to Spanish legend, is Jose Guirao Zamora?

Answers to Question Set 28

28-1) To get to the Magic Kingdom, guests usually travel over the Seven Seas Lagoon.

28-2) Sleeping Beauty is also known as Aurora and Briar Rose.

28-3) In her first appearance, Daisy Duck was referred to as Donna Duck.

28-4) Disney's barber shop quartet is called 'The Dapper Dans'.

28-5) Toy Story Land opened in November 2011 at Hong Kong Disneyland.

28-6) The two mice stars in 'Cinderella' are Gus and Jaq.

28-7) Mannequins, 8TRAX and the Neon Armadillo were all night clubs at Walt Disney World's Pleasure Island.

28-8) Walt based many of his ideas for Disneyland on Tivoli Gardens in Denmark, which he described as having a "happy and unbuttoned air of relaxed fun".

28-9) The 'Monsters, Inc.' prequel is called 'Monsters University' and shows Mike and Sulley's college years.

28-10) Jose Guirao Zamora was the name of a young boy from Mojacar, Spain, who was adopted by Elias and Flora Disney. He was given the American name 'Walter' and grew up as Walt Disney. Or at least, that's the story that the people of Mojacar tell to tourists, even though it has no basis in documented fact.

Question Set 29

29-1) What kind of animal is Pumbaa?

29-2) In which year did the Disney Cruise Line begin sailing?

29-3) On the Disney's Hollywood Studios Backlot Tour, which area shows the effects from a disaster movie?

29-4) Dame Julie Andrews played the part of Queen Clarisse Marie Renaldi in which Disney movies?

29-5) In the 'Cars' movies, who are the major sponsors of Lightning McQueen?

29-6) Which famous and celebrated film maker worked for Disney as an animator, storyboard artist and concept artist on 'The Fox and the Hound', 'The Black Cauldron' and 'Tron'?

29-7) Which boat is perched at the top of Mount Mayday in Typhoon Lagoon?

29-8) In 'The Emperor's New Groove', who is Yzma's henchman?

29-9) Who is 'Tarzan's elephant friend?

29-10) What is Disney's planned and guided travel company called?

Answers to Question Set 29

29-1) Pumbaa is a warthog.

29-2) The first Disney cruises were in 1998.

29-3) On the Disney's Hollywood Studios Backlot Tour, guests go through Catastrophe Canyon.

29-4) Dame Julie Andrews was the Queen in the 'Princess Diaries' movies.

29-5) Lightning McQueen drives for the Rust-Eze Medicated Bumper Ointment team.

29-6) Tim Burton began his film-making career as an animation apprentice in the early 1980's.

29-7) In Typhoon Lagoon, Miss Tilly is perched precariously at the top of Mount Mayday.

29-8) Kronk works for Yzma.

29-9) The elephant in 'Tarzan' is Tantor.

29-10) Disney's planned and guided travel company is 'Adventures By Disney'.

Question Set 30

30-1) In 'Beauty and the Beast', who voiced Mrs Potts?

30-2) What new musical, performed only on the Disney Cruise ships, is an original twist on the Cinderella story?

30-3) Which classic cartoon movie features 'the phoney King of England'?

30-4) When it was first built, what two things were technically unique about Walt Disney World's telephone system?

30-5) Who starred as Ernest P. Worrell in a series of Touchstone comedies?

30-6) 'A Dairy Tale' (a retelling of the Three Little Pigs story) is a short film spin-off of which Disney feature animation?

30-7) In 'Monsters, Inc.' what is the name of Mike's girlfriend?

30-8) What was the name of Walt Disney's brother, who ran the business side of the Disney company?

30-9) The son of the above Disney brother went on to be a long-time senior board member of the Disney company. Who was he?

30-10) In 'The Princess and the Frog', what is the name of the witchdoctor?

Answers to Question Set 30

30-1) Angela Lansbury was the voice of Mrs Potts.

30-2) 'Twice Charmed' – a musical play performing on the Disney Cruise Line ships – asks the question, "What if Cinderella's wicked stepsisters had another chance at marrying Prince Charming?"

30-3) The cowardly Prince John is 'the phoney King of England' in 'Robin Hood'.

30-4) Walt Disney World's telephone system was the first totally electronic system to use underground cable instead of overground poles, and the first to use fibre-optic cable.

30-5) Jim Varney was Ernest P. Worrell.

30-6) 'A Dairy Tale' features the stars of 'Home on the Range'.

30-7) In 'Monsters, Inc.' Mike's girlfriend is Celia Mae.

30-8) Walt's more financially aware brother was called Roy Oliver Disney.

30-9) Roy O. Disney's son was Roy Edward Disney.

30-10) The witchdoctor in 'The Princess and the Frog' is Dr Facilier, who some call The Shadow Man.

Question Set 31

31-1) 'There's a Great Big Beautiful Tomorrow' is the theme tune to which Disney attraction?

31-2) ...and which group recorded a version of it for the 'Meet the Robinsons' soundtrack?

31-3) Which classic Disney animation movie did Walt originally make as a Laugh-O-Gram short in 1922?

31-4) The 1987 Disney Channel four-part mini-series 'Anne of Avonlea' was a sequel to which classic tale?

31-5) On the Disney Cruise ships, which restaurant changes from black and white into colour throughout your meal?

31-6) What is Simba's evil uncle called in 'The Lion King'?

31-7) Who had his own TV series as 'The Science Guy' and also appears with Ellen in the Universe of Energy at EPCOT?

31-8) What kind of dog is Lady in 'Lady and the Tramp'?

31-9) Which real life boy looked after Winnie the Pooh?

31-10) In 'Enchanted', what was the name of Giselle's chipmunk friend?

Answers to Question Set 31

31-1) 'There's a Great Big Beautiful Tomorrow' is the theme tune to Walt Disney's Carousel of Progress.

31-2) They Might Be Giants sang 'There's a Great Big Beautiful Tomorrow' for the soundtrack of 'Meet the Robinsons'.

31-3) Walt's first version of 'Cinderella' was a Laugh-O-Gram short film in 1922.

31-4) 'Anne of Avonlea' was a sequel to 'Anne of Green Gables'.

31-5) The décor at the Animator's Palate restaurant is black and white when the starters are served, but has become glorious Technicolor by the time the coffee arrives.

31-6) Simba's evil uncle is called Scar.

31-7) Bill Nye is The Science Guy.

31-8) Lady is a cocker spaniel. Disney story man Joe Grant came up with the film's initial idea when he noticed how his own cocker spaniel, Lady, was shoved to one side when he and his wife had a new baby.

31-9) Winnie the Pooh belonged to Christopher Robin Milne, the son of author A. A. Milne.

31-10) The chipmunk in 'Enchanted' is called Pip.

Question Set 32

32-1) Disney made a series of 'D.A.R.E' educational films in the early nineties. What did D.A.R.E. stand for?

32-2) 'The Great Mouse Detective', Disney's 26th classic animation feature, was based on which book by Eve Titus?

32-3) Fred McMurray (1959) and Tim Allen (2006) starred in two different versions of which Disney movie?

32-4) At Disneyland, which hero has an adventure in the Temple of the Forbidden Eye?

32-5) What is the whale called in 'Pinocchio'?

32-6) What was the first 3D movie shown at EPCOT's Imagination! pavilion?

32-7) Disney's 1989 TV movie 'Danny, the Champion of the World' was based on a novel by which much-loved children's author?

32-8) Who voiced the role of Penny, 'Bolt' the wonder-dog's co-star?

32-9) Which hugely popular singing group got their first big break performing at Disneyland in 1961?

32-10) What are the names of the seven dwarfs?

Answers to Question Set 32

32-1) The D.A.R.E. films promoted Drug Abuse Resistance Education.

32-2) 'The Great Mouse Detective' was based on the book, 'Basil of Baker Street'.

32-3) Fred McMurray (1959) and Tim Allen (2006) starred in 'The Shaggy Dog'. Scott Weinger also took the lead in a 1994 TV movie version.

32-4) Disneyland's Indiana Jones adventure is in the Temple of the Forbidden Eye.

32-5) The whale that swallows Pinocchio is called Monstro.

32-6) 'Magic Journeys' was the Imagination! pavilion's first 3D movie.

32-7) Roald Dahl wrote 'Danny, the Champion of the World'.

32-8) In 'Bolt', Miley Cyrus played the part of Penny.

32-9) The Osmonds performed regularly at Disneyland in 1961, before appearing on the 'Disneyland After Dark' and 'Meet Me At Disneyland' TV shows.

32-10) The seven dwarfs are Happy, Dopey, Grumpy, Sleepy, Sneezy, Bashful and Doc.

Question Set 33

33-1) Where do baseball's Atlanta Braves hold there annual spring training camp?

33-2) Who is Buzz Lightyear's nemesis?

33-3) Remy the rat is the star of which movie?

33-4) Who is Stitch's musical hero?

33-5) In 1979 Disney released a live action family comedy about a group of traditional church ladies trying to drive some crooks out of their small town. Name either of the movie's two titles.

33-6) What is the name of the shopping and entertainment district that will replace Walt Disney World's Pleasure Island?

33-7) What is the submarine called in 'Atlantis: The Lost Empire'?

33-8) In 2005 who replaced Michael Eisner of C.E.O. of the Walt Disney Company?

33-9) Wayne Allwine and Russi Taylor were husband and wife, but in what capacities did they work for Disney?

33-10) Who is the old man in 'Up'?

Answers to Question Set 33

33-1) The Atlanta Braves hold there annual spring training camp at Walt Disney World's ESPN Wide World of Sports Complex.

33-2) Buzz Lightyear's arch-enemy is the Emperor Zurg.

33-3) Remy stars in 'Ratatouille'.

33-4) Stitch loves Elvis Presley.

33-5) 'The North Avenue Irregulars' was also released as 'Hill's Angels'.

33-6) Hyperion Wharf is to replace Pleasure Island at Walt Disney World.

33-7) In 'Atlantis: The Lost Empire', the submarine is called the Ulysses.

33-8) Robert Iger replaced Michael Eisner as Disney's C.E.O.

33-9) Wayne Allwine and Russi Taylor were the husband and wife team who provided the voices of Mickey and Minnie Mouse in the 'eighties and 'nineties.

33-10) 'Up' tells the story of Mr Carl Fredricksen and his flying house.

Question Set 34

34-1) Where is the Walt Disney Family Museum?

34-2) Which series of books by the author Margery Sharp formed the basis of two Disney animated movies?

34-3) In 'Sleeping Beauty', what are the names of the three fairies that help Aurora?

34-4) Which short film was Disney's first movie in colour?

34-5) Selena Gomez, David Henrie and Jake T. Austin were the stars of which Disney channel series?

34-6) Which animated series featured Bumblelion, Moosel, Rhinokey and Eleroo?

34-7) For his appearances in the theme parks, approximately how many costumes does Mickey Mouse have?

34-8) In what capacity did comedian and Disney Legend Steve Martin work for Disney at the age of ten?

34-9) What is WALL-E an abbreviation of?

34-10) What is the indoor interactive theme park (a virtual reality video game arcade with rides) at Walt Disney World's Downtown Disney called?

Answers to Question Set 34

34-1) The Walt Disney Family Museum is in the Presidio of San Francisco.

34-2) Margery Sharp wrote nine books about 'The Rescuers'.

34-3) 'Sleeping Beauty's three good fairies are Flora (who wears pink), Fauna (green) and Merryweather (blue).

34-4) Disney's first colour film was a Silly Symphony, 'Flowers and Trees', in 1932.

34-5) Selena Gomez, David Henrie and Jake T. Austin starred in 'Wizards of Waverly Place'.

34-6) Bumblelion, Moosel, Rhinokey and Eleroo were some of 'The Wuzzles'.

34-7) Mickey has over 325 different costumes to choose from.

34-8) The ten year old Steve Martin sold guide books at Disneyland after school. He continued working at the park for eight years, three of them demonstrating and selling magic tricks.

34-9) WALL-E is a **W**aste **A**llocation **L**oad **L**ifter – **E**arth Class.

34-10) Florida's indoor interactive theme park is called Disney Quest.

Question Set 35

35-1) Located on Florida's Atlantic coast, what was the first Disney Vacation Club site to be built outside of the theme park resorts?

35-2) What is the name of the little Hawaiian girl who befriends the alien Stitch?

35-3) What is the name of the little Japanese girl who befriends the alien Stitch in the 'Stitch!' TV series?

35-4) Where on Disney property can you stay overnight in a jail, saloon or other wild west-styled buildings?

35-5) What is Minnie Mouse's mischievous sister called?

35-6) Which famous wrestler played a taxi driver in 'Race to Witch Mountain'?

35-7) Who are Ursula's two eel henchmen in 'The Little Mermaid'?

35-8) Which famous American country singer and actor from the 1930's reprised one of his most famous songs as the voice of Big Al in the Country Bear Jamboree?

35-9) What was Pixar's first feature length movie?

35-10) ...and what was its first ever short film?

Answers to Question Set 35

35-1) The first Disney Vacation Club site outside of a theme park area was at Vero Beach, Florida.

35-2) When he first comes to Earth, Stitch is befriended by Lilo Pelekai.

35-3) In the anime TV series, Stitch finds a new friend in Yuna Kamihara (who was called Hanako during the program's writing and development). By the internal timeline of this series Lilo is now grown up and has a daughter of her own.

35-4) The Hotel Cheyenne at Disneyland Paris has a cowboy theme and is based upon a town from the 'wild west'.

35-5) Minnie's naughty sister is Mandie Mouse.

35-6) Dwayne 'The Rock' Johnson played taxi driver Jack Bruno in 'Race to Witch Mountain' in 2009.

35-7) The two eels in 'The Little Mermaid' are Flotsam and Jetsam.

35-8) Tex Ritter voiced Big Al in the Country Bear Jamboree.

35-9) Pixar's first full length feature was 'Toy Story'.

35-10) Pixar's first short film, made in 1984, was 'The Adventures of André and Wally B.'

Question Set 36

36-1) Which classic Disney live action / cartoon hybrid feature has never been released on video or DVD in the United States?

36-2) At the Tokyo Disney Resort, what is Ikspiari?

36-3) What is Nahtazu?

36-4) Which lazy but incredibly lucky goose is Donald Duck's cousin?

36-5) A bunker on the 6th hole of which Disney golf course is designed to look like Mickey's head?

36-6) Who is Jake Long?

36-7) Which Pixar movie has a plot loosely based on 'The Seven Samurai'?

36-8) What is the name of the black panther in 'The Jungle Book'?

36-9) Whose book – 'Work In Progress'– related to their time at Disney?

36-10) Where in Walt Disney World can you find 12 statues representing Adventure, Compassion, Discovery, Freedom, Heritage, Independence, Individualism, Innovation, Knowledge, Pioneering, Self-Reliance and Tomorrow?

Answers to Question Set 36

36-1) 'Song of the South' has yet to be made available for legal home viewing in the USA.

36-2) Ikspiari is Tokyo Disneyland's shopping, dining and entertainment district; the equivalent of Downtown Disney.

36-3) According to an advertising campaign, Disney's Animal Kingdom is 'Nahtazu' – because it's 'not-a-zoo'.

36-4) Donald's lucky cousin is Gladstone Gander.

36-5) The famous Mickey-shaped sand trap is at the Magnolia course at Walt Disney World.

36-6) Jake Long is the animated star of 'American Dragon'.

36-7) 'A Bug's Life' shares many plot similarities with 'The Seven Samurai'.

36-8) 'The Jungle Book's black panther is called Bagheera.

36-9) 'Work in Progress' is a memoir by former Disney CEO Michael Eisner.

36-10) The 12 inspirational statues can be seen down the sides of the theatre in 'The American Adventure'.

Question Set 37

37-1) Whose name is on the NASCAR racetrack at Walt Disney World?

37-2) Who, along with his friend Luna, finished every episode of his TV show with The Goodbye Song?

37-3) Daphne Blunt stars in which Radio Disney serial?

37-4) Which 1970's pop legend sang I'll Make a Man Out of You on the 'Mulan' soundtrack?

37-5) ...and which oriental superstar dubbed the singing voice for the Mandarin Chinese version of the movie?

37-6) What was the previous name of Disneyland's Critter Country?

37-7) Which 1964 movie starring Tommy Kirk and Annette Funicello led to a sequel called 'The Monkey's Uncle'?

37-8) Which character was Scrooge McDuck's pilot in 'Duck Tales' and was also Darkwing Duck's sidekick?

37-9) Which famous singer performed seven songs for 'Piglet's Big Movie'?

37-10) Which horse character from the early Mickey Mouse short films and comics was occasionally shown as the fiancé of Clarabelle Cow?

Answers to Question Set 37

37-1) You can drive a NASCAR race car at the Richard Petty Driving Experience at Walt Disney World.

37-2) 'The Bear in the Big Blue House' sang The Goodbye Song.

37-3) 'My Dream' is a Radio Disney serial starring Daphne Blunt as a girl trying to become a famous singer.

37-4) In the American version of 'Mulan', I'll Make a Man Out of You is sung by Donny Osmond.

37-5) ...but in the Chinese version the song is sung by the actor Jackie Chan who played the voice of Li Shang for the Chinese version of the movie.

37-6) Critter Country at Disneyland was previously known as Bear Country.

37-7) 'The Monkey's Uncle' was a sequel to 'The Misadventures of Merlin Jones'.

37-8) Launchpad McQuack was Uncle Scrooge's pilot and also Darkwing Duck's sidekick. He proudly proclaimed, 'If it's got wings, I can crash it'. He was also a scoutmaster of Huey, Dewey and Louie's Junior Woodchucks troop.

37-9) Carly Simon performed most of the soundtrack for 'Piglet's Big Movie'.

37-10) Clarabelle Cow's fiancé was Horace Horsecollar.

Question Set 38

38-1) Which former Beatle recorded a version of the song, When You Wish Upon a Star?

38-2) What are Cinderella's ugly stepsisters called?

38-3) In the Orlando area, what is Mickey's Retreat?

38-4) Who starred as 'Dick Tracy' in the 1990 Touchstone movie?

38-5) Which series of videos, DVDs and laserdiscs allowed viewers to 'follow the bouncing Mickey' in karaoke versions for Disney classic musical moments?

38-6) In 'The Aristocats', what classic song does Scat Cat sing?

38-7) Where could you have watched the 'Voyage of the Ghost Ship'?

38-8) Which ill-fated Disneyland ride took just three minutes to run the same track that the PeopleMover had covered in sixteen minutes?

38-9) Who raises Quasimodo in 'The Hunchback of Notre Dame'?

38-10) Who are Aquata, Andrina, Arista, Attina, Adella and Alana?

Answers to Question Set 38

38-1) Ringo Starr recorded When You Wish Upon a Star for the 1988 various artists album Stay Awake.

38-2) Lady Tremaine's daughters are Drizella and Anastasia.

38-3) Mickey's Retreat at Little Lake Bryan near Downtown Disney is a cast members-only recreation area where Disney staff and their families can relax away from the tourist crowds.

38-4) Warren Beatty was 'Dick Tracy'.

38-5) The series of over thirty Disney karaoke home videos were called 'Sing Along Songs'.

38-6) Scatman Crothers sings 'Ev'rybody Wants to be a Cat' as Scat Cat in 'The Aristocats'.

38-7) 'Voyage of the Ghost Ship' was a Broadway-style stage show performed on the Disney Magic and Disney Wonder cruise ships

38-8) Rocket Rods ran for just two and a half years at Disneyland. It covered the same track that the PeopleMover had run on for 28 years.

38-9) The young Quasimodo is raised by the villainous Judge Claude Frollo.

38-10) Aquata, Andrina, Arista, Attina, Adella and Alana are Ariel's sisters, the Daughters of Triton from 'The Little Mermaid'.

Question Set 39

39-1) What is the name of Maleficent's pet raven?

39-2) Which 1993 movie told a fictionalised version of the story of the 1988 Winter Olympic Jamaican bobsled team?

39-3) In which Disney park can you see Mickey's Jammin' Jungle Parade?

39-4) Where can you play a game of miniature golf on the Goofy Golf course?

39-5) In which full length animated movie does the character Ffewddur Fflam appear?

39-6) Victoria and Albert's, the restaurant at Disney's Grand Floridian resort, employs Disney's only full-time player of which musical instrument?

39-7) Off which Interstate Highway does Disneyland lie?

39-8) ...and which Interstate leads to Walt Disney World?

39-9) Milo Fishtooth, Oscar Fishtooth and Bea Goldfishberg were the main characters in which Disney Channel animated series?

39-10) Who was Nemo's mother?

Answers to Question Set 39

39-1) Maleficent's raven is called Diablo.

39-2) The 1988 Winter Olympic Jamaican bobsled team featured in 'Cool Runnings'.

39-3) Mickey's Jammin' Jungle Parade runs through Disney's Animal Kingdom park.

39-4) The Goofy Golf course is on board the Disney Dream cruise ship.

39-5) Ffewddur Fflam is voiced by Nigel Havers in 'The Black Cauldron'.

39-6) Victoria and Albert's at Disney's Grand Floridian resort employs the company's only full-time harpist.

39-7) Disneyland is close to Interstate 5.

39-8) ...while I4 leads to Walt Disney World, just west of the Florida Turnpike.

39-9) Milo, Oscar and Bea were the lead characters in 'Fish Hooks'.

39-10) Nemo's mother was called Pearl.

Question Set 40

40-1) Sting sings My Funny Friend and Me over the end credits of which animated movie?

40-2) The Tower of Terror ride takes its theming from which sixties TV series?

40-3) What is the murderous leopard called in 'Tarzan'?

40-4) Who is Lucky the Dinosaur?

40-5) What is the name of the demon from 'Fantasia's Night on Bald Mountain segment?

40-6) Who narrates the 2011 'Winnie the Pooh' movie?

40-7) What is the full name of the tow truck in the 'Cars' movies?

40-8) ...and what is his spin-off series of short films called?

40-9) What is Prince Eric's dog called in 'The Little Mermaid'?

40-10) Hayley Mills and Hayley Mills (as identical twins) sing Let's Get Together in which Disney movie?

Answers to Question Set 40

40-1) Sting sings My Funny Friend and Me in 'The Emperor's New Groove'.

40-2) The Tower of Terror ride is themed to take riders into an episode of 'The Twilight Zone'.

40-3). Sabor the leopard killed Tarzan's parents and Kala's infant son

40-4) Lucky the Dinosaur is Disney's first free-walking audio-animatronic figure. He is eight feet high, green, he pulls a cart filled with flowers and (along with his friend Chandler the Handler) was a fairly regular feature in the American Disney parks in 2005. At the time of writing Lucky and Chandler are 'resting'.

40-5) 'Fantasia's demon is called Chernabog.

40-6) John Cleese is the narrator of 'Winnie the Pooh'.

40-7) The tow truck in 'Cars' is called Sir Tow Mater.

40-8) He is the star of the 'Cars Toons: Mater's Tall Tales' series.

40-9) The dog in 'The Little Mermaid' is called Max.

40-10) Hayley Mills played both identical twins Susan Evers and Sharon McKendrick in 'The Parent Trap'.

Question Set 41

41-1) Which character has the head structure and horns of a buffalo, the arms and body of a bear, the eyebrows of a gorilla, the jaws, teeth, and mane of a lion, the tusks of a wild boar and the legs and tail of a wolf?

41-2) Who is the conductor in 'Fantasia 2000'?

41-3) Where does Disney provide a safe saltwater reef populated with stingrays, shovelhead sharks, leopard sharks and tropical fish for guests to swim through with the aid of snorkels?

41-4) Which Disney night-time show takes its name from a 1960's television series?

41-5) Which comedy horror movie starring Jeff Daniels and John Goodman was Disney's first release under the more adult Hollywood Pictures banner?

41-6) Who portrays the voice of Queen Clarion in 'Tinker Bell' and 'Tinker Bell and the Lost Treasure'?

41-7) Who was our guide in the short series of educational movies 'You and Your...'?

41-8) What was Disney's first roller coaster to feature a loop?

41-9) In which classic short film does Mickey Mouse enter a strange world where he dances with an enthusiastic pair of gloves and an entire pack of animated cards (including a jealous King)?

41-10) Where on Disney property could you celebrate New Year every night?

Answers to Question Set 41

41-1) The Beast is an amalgam of parts from a buffalo, a bear, a gorilla, a lion, a wild boar and a wolf.

41-2) James Levine conducted the Chicago Symphony Orchestra on the soundtrack of 'Fantasia 2000'.

41-3) Guests can get in the water with stingrays and sharks at Typhoon Lagoon's Shark Reef.

41-4) The nightly show at Disney's California Adventure is called 'World of Color'.

41-5) Jeff Daniels and John Goodman were the stars of 'Arachnophobia'.

41-6) In 'Tinker Bell' and 'Tinker Bell and the Lost Treasure', Queen Clarion is voiced by Anjelica Huston.

41-7) Jiminy Cricket explained our ears, our eyes etc in the 'You and Your...' series.

41-8) Disney's first looping coaster was Indiana Jones et le Temple du Péril at Disneyland Paris. In later years they adapted the ride so that it ran backwards.

41-9) Mickey has adventures on the other side of the looking glass in 'Thru the Mirror'.

41-10) There was a New Years Eve party every night at Walt Disney World's Pleasure Island.

Question Set 42

42-1) Which character from 'The Sword in the Stone' describes herself in song as magnificent, marvellous and mad?

42-2) Which 'High School Musical' spin-off movie starred Ashley Tisdale as the title character?

42-3) When did the Disney Channel begin broadcasting in the U.S.?

42-4) Which nightly theme park show ends with Mickey slaying the dragon Maleficent?

42-5) Bette Midler, Kathy Najimy and Sarah Jessica Parker starred as three witches – The Sanderson Sisters – in which spooky movie from 1993?

42-6) Where and when in EPCOT could guests experience the sounds of the Brazilian rain forest, play a round of mini-golf and walk the streets of Jerusalem (via real imported paving stones)?

42-7) What kind of creatures are Rutt and Tuke in 'Brother Bear'?

42-8) Who is the villain in 'The Incredibles'?

42-9) Which Disney song features the line 'Salagadoola mechicka boola'?

42-10) Which movie based on a Disney theme park attraction featured the singing voices of Don Henley, Bonnie Raitt and John Hiatt?

Answers to Question Set 42

42-1) Merlin's nemesis in 'The Sword in the Stone' is the magnificent, marvellous, mad Madam Mim.

42-2) Ashley Tisdale was the star of 'Sharpay's Fabulous Adventure'.

42-3) The Disney Channel launched at 7a.m. on April 18, 1983 with a compilation of short cartoons called 'Good Morning Mickey'.

42-4) Mickey slays the dragon at the end of Fantasmic!

42-5) The Sanderson Sisters appeared in 'Hocus Pocus'.

42-6) EPCOT guests could experience many new things in the Millennium Village, which opened on October 1, 1999 and stayed open throughout the whole of 2000.

42-7) Rutt and Tuke are Canadian moose.

42-8) The bad guy in 'The Incredibles' is Syndrome.

42-9) Cinderella's Bibbidi-Bobbidi-Boo starts with the words 'Salagadoola mechicka boola'.

42-10) Don Henley, Bonnie Raitt and John Hiatt provided singing voices for 'The Country Bears' movie.

Question Set 43

43-1) In 'Finding Nemo', what does Dory suffer from?

43-2) Which 1969 live action comedy spawned two sequels called 'Now You See Him Now You Don't' and 'The Strongest Man in the World'?

43-3) At Tokyo Disneyland, what it the name of the Tower of Terror hotel?

43-4) In Aladdin, what is the name of Jafar's parrot?

43-5) In the late 'nineties Disney opened five children's play centres, or 'imagination-powered playsites'. What was their collective name?

43-6) Sir Michael Caine provided the voice for which British secret agent in 'Cars 2'?

43-7) Sports stars Shaquille O'Neal, Ken Griffey Jr., Wayne Gretzky, Joe Montana, Monica Seles and Andre Agassi all invested in which establishment at Walt Disney World?

43-8) What is the name of the alligator in 'The Princess and the Frog'?

43-9) Whose tooth provided the title of an early Disney educational film?

43-10) Which of Donald Duck's uncles is described as a scientist, lecturer, psychologist, and road traveler?

Answers to Question Set 43

43-1) Dory is a Pacific regal blue tang who suffers from short-term memory loss.

43-2) 'Now You See Him, Now You Don't' and 'The Strongest Man in the World' were sequels to 'The Computer Wore Tennis Shoes'.

43-3) Tokyo's version of the Tower of Terror ride is housed within the Hotel Hightower, as opposed to The Hollywood Tower hotel theming of the rides in Florida, California and Paris. There are no references to 'The Twilight Zone' on the Tokyo ride as the show wasn't shown much in Japan and therefore mentioning it wouldn't have the same cultural impact as in other parts of the world.

43-4) The parrot in Aladdin is named Iago.

43-5) Disney's failed imagination-powered playsites were called Club Disney. All had closed within four years of the first one's opening.

43-6) In 'Cars 2' Sir Michael Caine plays Finn McMissile.

43-7) Various sports stars invested in the Official All Star Café at Disney's Wide World of Sports complex.

43-8) 'The Princess and the Frog's trumpet playing alligator is called Louis.

43-9) A Kansas city dentist commissioned the young Walt Disney to produce an educational movie called 'Tommy Tucker's Tooth'.

43-10) Donald's uncle Ludwig von Drake is a scientist, lecturer, psychologist, and road traveler.

Question Set 44

44-1) Buck Cluck is the father of which Disney hero?

44-2) Where is The Earful Tower?

44-3) What was the Disney family's poodle called?

44-4) The Jonas Brothers' TV series 'Jonas' was renamed for its second season to reflect the brothers' move to which American city?

44-5) Who can you 'talk turtle' with at the Disney theme parks?

44-6) In 'Up', which Wilderness Explorer badge is the little boy, Russell, trying to earn?

44-7) What is Winter Summerland?

44-8) Sir Tim Rice and Elton John wrote which Disney stage musical?

44-9) Which controversial character was played by James Baskett?

44-10) Which permanent Disneyland Paris show features Donald dancing with a quartet of Pink Elephants in a show full of UV light and fluorescent paint effects?

Answers to Question Set 44

44-1) Buck Cluck is 'Chicken Little's dad.

44-2) The Earful Tower is the water tower at Disney's Hollywood Studios. A similar tower at Disneyland Paris is called the Earffel Tower.

44-3) Walt and his family had a poodle called Lady.

44-4) The Jonas Brothers' show was renamed 'Jonas L.A.'.

44-5) Guests can talk turtle with Crush from 'Finding Nemo' in an interactive live show.

44-6) In 'Up', Russell is trying to get his Assisting the Elderly badge.

44-7) Winter Summerland is a miniature golf course at Walt Disney World.

44-8) Sir Tim Rice and Elton John wrote 'Elaborate Lives: The Legend Of Aida' – later shortened to simply 'Aida'.

44-9) James Baskett played Uncle Remus in 'Song of the South'.

44-10) Donald dances with Pink Elephants in the Animagique show at Disneyland Paris.

Question Set 45

45-1) Where can you hear the band Off Kilter play music several times a day?

45-2) Which Disney teen sitcom featured an animated version of the live action title character speaking her thoughts directly to the audience?

45-3) Kala is the adopted mother of which Disney title hero?

45-4) Who provided the voice of Mickey Mouse in his earliest movies?

45-5) Who played The White Queen in the 2010 live action version of 'Alice in Wonderland'?

45-6) Where can you get sustenance at Frostbite Freddie's, Avalunch and the Polar Pub?

45-7) What was the sequel to 'A Goofy Movie'?

45-8) Which infant was Roger Rabbit's comedy partner?

45-9) The Widow Tweed and Amos Slade look after which Disney duo?

45-10) k.d.lang sang 'Little Patch of Heaven' in which animated movie?

Answers to Question Set 45

45-1) The Celtic rock band Off Kilter perform daily at the Canada pavilion in EPCOT's World Showcase.

45-2) The live action/animation hybrid sitcom was 'Lizzie McGuire'.

45-3) Kala is the gorilla who raises 'Tarzan'.

45-4) Walt Disney himself originally provided Mickey's voice.

45-5) In Tim Burton's 2010 version of 'Alice in Wonderland, Anne Hathaway played Mirana of Marmoreal, the White Queen.

45-6) Frostbite Freddie's, Avalunch and the Polar Pub are all at Disney's Blizzard Beach water park.

45-7) 'A Goofy Movie' was followed by 'An Extremely Goofy Movie'.

45-8) Roger Rabbit was teamed up with Baby Herman.

45-9) The Widow Tweed raises Tod and Amos Slade owns Copper in 'The Fox and the Hound'.

45-10) 'Little Patch of Heaven' features in 'Home on the Range'.

Question Set 46

46-1) As what was Disney's Hollywood Studios theme park previously known?

46-2) What is the sequel to the live action '101 Dalmatians' called?

46-3) And what was the title of the direct to video sequel to the original animated '101 Dalmatians'?

46-4) Who provides the love interest for 'Hercules'?

46-5) Who has friends called Ratty, Moley and Angus McBadger?

46-6) 'The Pumpkin King' and 'Oogie's Revenge' are video games based on which Disney movie?

46-7) At EPCOT, what can be seen in coral, teal, lime, gold and peach versions?

46-8) What was the Disney TV series that featured the childhood lives of the animal characters from 'The Jungle Book'?

46-9) What is the name of Bambi's mate?

46-10) In the film 'Bolt', what kind of creature is the character Rhino?

Answers to Question Set 46

46-1) The Disney's Hollywood Studios theme park opened on May 1, 1989 as Disney-MGM Studios. It changed its name in January 2008.

46-2) Glenn Close starred in '101 Dalmatians' and its sequel, '102 Dalmatians'.

46-3) In 2003 Disney belatedly followed up 1961's animated classic '101 Dalmatians' with a sequel, '101 Dalmatians II: Patch's London Adventure'.

46-4) Hercules falls in love with Megara, usually shortened to Meg.

46-5) Ratty, Moley and Angus McBadger are friends of J. Thaddeus Toad, Esq., the reckless Mr. Toad of Toad Hall.

46-6) The games 'The Pumpkin King' and 'Oogie's Revenge' are based on 'The Nightmare Before Christmas'.

46-7) The EPCOT monorails are all identified by their livery colour, including coral, teal, lime, gold and peach.

46-8) The young animals from 'The Jungle Book' were the stars of 'Jungle Cubs'.

46-9) Bambi falls in love with Faline.

46-10) In 'Bolt', Rhino is a fearless hamster.

Question Set 47

47-1) Bubbles, Chuchie, Do and Aqua were members of which band, according to a Disney Channel movie?

47-2) Galen Bradwarden killed the 400 year old Vermithrax Pejorative in which 1981 fantasy movie, co-produced by Disney and Paramount?

47-3) What are Bob and Helen Parr and their children collectively known as?

47-4) The outside of which Walt Disney World attraction is a pentakis dodecahedron made up of 11,324 silvered facets, with 954 partial or full flat triangular panels?

47-5) Which 1967 book by Daniel P. Mannix became a Disney animated feature film 14 years after its publication?

47-6) Before she met John Smith, which Native American Powhatan warrior was Pocahontas destined to marry?

47-7) Who is known in Italy as Topolino?

47-8) Who, in 1987, was the first person honoured with a Disney Legend award?

47-9) In which EPCOT attraction could guests select from a choice of ride endings while travelling sideways?

47-10) What is Disney's Hawaiian resort called?

Answers to Question Set 47

47-1) Bubbles, Chuchie, Do and Aqua were the Cheetah Girls.

47-2) Vermithrax Pejorative was the impressive dragon in 'Dragonslayer'.

47-3) Bob, Helen, Dashiell, Violet and Jack-Jack Parr are 'The Incredibles'.

47-4) Geometrically, EPCOT's Spaceship Earth is a pentakis dodecahedron.

47-5) Daniel P. Mannix wrote the book, 'The Fox and The Hound'.

47-6) The warrior Kocoum wishes to marry Pocahontas.

47-7) In Italy, Mickey Mouse is known as Topolino. It literally translates as 'baby mouse'.

47-8) The actor Fred McMurray was the first recipient of the Disney Legend award.

47-9) Guests could pick their own ending while riding EPCOT's Horizons.

47-10) Disney's resort in Hawaii is named Aulani.

Question Set 48

48-1) Eglantine Price and Emelius Browne search for the Star of Astoroth in which Disney movie?

48-2) What was the one million point prize in the Who Wants to Be a Millionaire – Play It! theme park attraction?

48-3) What was Pixar's first TV series called?

48-4) Which Disney ride vehicle was piloted by the robot RX-24, or Rex for short?

48-5) French crooner Maurice Chevalier sang the theme tune to which animated Disney movie??

48-6) BeamWars, Deadly Discs and Battle Grids are video games based on which Disney franchise?

48-7) The Jonas Brothers and Demi Lovato starred in which Disney Channel original movie and its sequel?

48-8) Where are the Kali River Rapids?

48-9) What are the C.K. Holliday, E.P. Ripley, Fred Gurley, Ernest S. Marsh and Ward Kimball?

48-10) Darwin, Blaster and Juarez are FBI Special Agents in which division?

Answers to Question Set 48

48-1) Miss Price and Professor Browne appear in 'Bedknobs and Broomsticks'.

48-2) Guests could win a Disney cruise for four people on Who Wants to Be a Millionaire – Play It! along with a leather jacket.

48-3) Pixar's first television series was 'Buzz Lightyear of Star Command'.

48-4) RX-24 (AKA Rex) was the unwilling pilot of the Starspeeder 3000 ride vehicle in the original Star Tours attraction.

48-5) Maurice Chevalier sang the theme song for 'The Aristocats'.

48-6) BeamWars, Deadly Discs and Battle Grids are all set in the world of 'Tron'.

48-7) The Jonas Brothers and Demi Lovato were the stars of 'Camp Rock'.

48-8) The Kali River Rapids are in the Asia section of Disney's Animal Kingdom.

48-9) C.K. Holliday, E.P. Ripley, Fred Gurley, Ernest S. Marsh and Ward Kimball are all locomotives on the Disneyland railroad.

48-10) Darwin, Blaster and Juarez are part of the FBI's 'G-Force' squad.

Question Set 49

49-1) In which movie does Burl Ives sing The Ugly Bug Ball?

49-2) 'Little Britain' star Matt Lucas played which characters in Tim Burton's live action 'Alice In Wonderland?

49-3) In 'Fantasia 2000', which Disney character herded animals into an ark to save them from a great flood?

49-4) Which Disney theatrical production which had runs in California and New York, is a prequel to 'Peter Pan'?

49-5) 'Mickey and the Beanstalk' formed part of which full-length movie?

49-6) Which of the early EPCOT pavilions closed its doors for good on January 1st 2007?

49-7) What are the two Disney parks in Paris called?

49-8) In 'The Rescuers', who is abducted from the Morningside Orphanage?

49-9) Which classic animated movie contains the songs I'm in a World of my Own, Old Father William and The Caucus Race?

49-10) Marc Okrand, who had created the Klingon language for 'Star Trek', developed a new language for which Disney movie?

Answers to Question Set 49

49-1) Burl Ives sang The Ugly Bug Ball in the Hayley Mill's movie, 'Summer Magic'.

49-2) Matt Lucas appeared as both Tweedledum and Tweedledee.

49-3) In 'Fantasia 2000' Donald Duck took on the role of the biblical Noah.

49-4) 'Peter and the Starcatcher' is a prequel to 'Peter Pan'.

49-5) 'Mickey and the Beanstalk' was a portion of the 1947 release, 'Fun and Fancy Free'.

49-6) The Wonders of Life pavilion closed at the start of 2007.

49-7) Disney's Parisian theme parks are Disneyland Park and the Walt Disney Studios Park.

49-8) Penny was the little girl who lived at the Morningside Orphanage.

49-9) I'm in a World of my Own, Old Father William and The Caucus Race all feature in 'Alice in Wonderland'.

49-10) Disney commissioned Marc Okrand to develop an Atlantean language for 'Atlantis: The Lost Empire'.

Question Set 50

50-1) Who was the human owner of the 'Toy Story' toys?

50-2) What colour noses do the chipmunks Chip an' Dale have?

50-3) What is the name of Captain Jack Sparrow's ship in the 'Pirates of the Caribbean' movies?

50-4) ...and what was the ship's previous name?

50-5) Where might you see Waldo C. Graphic?

50-6) Where is Disney's Hollywood Hotel?

50-7) Which animated movie's trio of heroines are named Maggie, Mrs Calloway and Grace?

50-8) Adriana Caselotti was the voice of which Disney Princess?

50-9) What was Eddie Murphy's character's job in 'The Haunted Mansion'?

50-10) In which movie did Kirk Douglas sing 'A Whale of a Tale'?

Answers to Question Set 50

50-1) Buzz, Woody and the other toys belonged to Andy Davis.

50-2) Chip's nose is black (like a chocolate chip), while Dale's is a chestnut reddish brown.

50-3) Jack Sparrow was captain of The Black Pearl

50-4) The Black Pearl was previously named Wicked Wench, which is the name of a ship in the Disneyland attraction.

50-5) Waldo C. Graphic is a computer-generated character in Jim Henson's Muppet*Vision 3D at the Disney theme parks.

50-6) Disney's Hollywood Hotel is at Hong Kong Disneyland. It's name is frequently confused with the Hollywood Tower Hotel, Walt Disney World's Tower of Terror.

50-7) Maggie, Mrs Calloway and Grace are the three cows from 'Home on the Range'.

50-8) Adriana Caselotti was the voice of 'Snow White'. Under the terms of her contract she was allowed to do very little other work, as Walt Disney said, "I'm sorry, but that voice can't be used anywhere. I don't want to spoil the illusion of Snow White."

50-9) In 'The Haunted Mansion' Eddie Murphy played Jim Evers, a real estate agent. His sales pitch is 'At Evers & Evers, we want you to be satisfied for evers and evers'.

50-10) Kirk Douglas sang A Whale of a Tale in '20,000 Leagues Under the Sea'.

Question Set 51

51-1) Which Disney Channel series is about a teenage actor who stars as a secret agent on a fictional TV show called 'Silverstone'?

51-2) Which Disneyland ride took its name from a character from 'Chip 'n' Dale Rescue Rangers'?

51-3) In Toy Story 3, what is the day care centre that the toys go to called?

51-4) Who were Practical, Fiddler and Fifer?

51-5) Who was the first serving American President to provide his own voice for The Hall of Presidents?

51-6) What did the 70 year old Tiny Kline become the first person to do in 1961? It was something that she continued to do at Disneyland on most nights for the next three years?

51-7) What was the first official cruise line of Walt Disney World?

51-8) What was the original name of the hockey team in 'The Mighty Ducks'?

51-9) Stitch's Great Escape! replaced which previous theatre-in-the-round attraction at Walt Disney World?

51-10) Which American pop trio released a '3D Concert Experience' movie in 2009?

Answers to Question Set 51

51-1) The star of 'Silverstone' is 'The Famous Jett Jackson'.

51-2) 'Chip 'n' Dale Rescue Rangers' provided the theming for Gadget's Go Coaster.

51-3) Much of 'Toy Story 3' is set in Sunnyside Daycare.

51-4) Practical, Fiddler and Fifer were 'The Three Little Pigs' who starred in their own series of Silly Symphonies.

51-5) The first President to provide his voice for the Hall of Presidents while still in office was Bill Clinton.

51-6) Tiny Kline was the first person to 'fly' as Tinker Bell during Disneyland's nightly fireworks display.

51-7) Before launching their own cruise ships, Disney had an agreement with the Premier Cruise Line to provide land and sea vacation packages and use the trademark 'The Big Red Boat'.

51-8) District 5 ice hockey team became 'The Mighty Ducks'.

51-9) Stitch's Great Escape! operates where the ExtraTERRORestrial Alien Encounter once played.

51-10) Disney's 2009 movie was called 'Jonas Brothers: The 3D Concert Experience'.

Question Set 52

52-1) What are the two names of the male hero in Disney's 'Tangled'?

52-2) What is Jiko at the Animal Kingdom Lodge resort?

52-3) Lightning McQueen finds himself in which small town in 'Cars'?

52-4) Everyone knows that 'Snow White' was Disney's first full-length animated feature film, but what was the second?

52-5) In 2010 Cinderella's Golden Carrousel in Florida's Magic Kingdom changed its name. What to?

52-6) What was the very first animated 3D cartoon?

52-7) Which tunnelling character, introduced in 'Winnie the Pooh and the Honey Tree', was not in the books by A. A .Milne?

52-8) Which ride, unique to the Tokyo DisneySea theme park, is based on a book by Jules Verne?

52-9) Where in Walt Disney World can guests eat dinner while sitting in cars in a drive-in movie theatre?

52-10) Brenda Song stars as which Homecoming Warrior in a Disney Channel original movie?

Answers to Question Set 52

52-1) Rapunzel's love interest in 'Tangled' is Eugene Fitzhubert, also known as Flynn Rider.

52-2) Jiko is a restaurant. Its name means The Cooking Place in Swahili.

52-3) 'Cars' is set in the town of Radiator Springs.

52-4) 'Pinocchio' was Disney's second full-length animated movie.

52-5) The name was changed from Cinderella's Golden Carrousel to Prince Charming Regal Carrousel.

52-6) The first 3D cartoon was 'Adventures in Music: Melody' in 1953. It was followed a few months later by the Chip 'n' Dale 3D short, 'Working for Peanuts'.

52-7) A. A. Milne never wrote about Samuel J. Gopher.

52-8) Tokyo DisneySea is the only place that guests can take the Journey to the Center of the Earth.

52-9) The Sci-Fi Dine In restaurant at the Disney's Hollywood Studios is themed like a drive-in movie theatre.

52-10) Brenda Song played 'Wendy Wu: Homecoming Warrior'.

Question Set 53

53-1) 'Take Down', a family drama set in the world of high school wrestling, was the first Disney movie to be awarded what?

53-2) At Walt Disney World, what were Crocodile Belle, Darting Dragonfly, Hasty Hippo, Leaping Lizard and Otter Nonsense?

53-3) What was the first animated film ever to be nominated for the Best Movie Oscar?

53-4) Chester and Hester are the proprietors of which portion of Disney's Animal Kingdom?

53-5) Who played the voice of 'Kim Possible's friend, Monique?

53-6) From 2005 to 2008 Disney ran an online video game called VMK with a twist that players could earn bonuses by completing missions in the real life theme parks. What did VMK stand for?

53-7) Which 1960 Disney movie tells the story of John Wesley Powell and his 1869 expedition to map the Colorado River?

53-8) Initially only printed with the numbers one or five, what did Disneyland and Walt Disney World start issuing in 1987?

53-9) Singer/songwriter Melissa Etheridge contributed three songs to which animated movie sequel?

53-10) It's Fun to Be Free was the theme tune for which EPCOT attraction which closed in 1996?

Answers to Question Set 53

53-1) Released in 1979, 'Take Down' was the first Disney movie to receive a PG rating.

53-2) Crocodile Belle, Darting Dragonfly, Hasty Hippo, Leaping Lizard and Otter Nonsense were the vessels on the Animal Kingdom's short-lived Discovery River Boats ride.

53-3) 'Beauty and the Beast' was the first animated film ever to be nominated for the Best Movie Oscar. It lost out to 'The Silence of the Lambs'.

53-4) Chester and Hester are the fictional owners of DinoLand U.S.A.

53-5) 'Kim Possible's friend, Monique was voiced by Raven-Symoné of 'That's So Raven' fame.

53-6) VMK was the Virtual Magic Kingdom.

53-7) John Wesley Powell's 1869 expedition was depicted in 'Ten Who Dared'.

53-8) Disney Dollars were first issued (in one dollar and five dollar denominations) in 1987.

53-9) Melissa Etheridge sang three songs for the soundtrack of 'Brother Bear II'.

53-10) It's Fun to Be Free was the theme tune for World of Motion.

Question Set 54

54-1) What is the abominable snowman on Disneyland's Matterhorn Bobsleds ride called?

54-2) The Brazilian parrot José Carioca appeared in which two Disney feature movies?

54-3) Milo Kamalani and Nicky Little attend Hazelnut Middle School along with their friend, the title character of which Disney animated TV series?

54-4) Which animated movie featured a Scottish terrier called Jock and a bloodhound named Trusty?

54-5) Which resort and learning centre formerly operated on the site of Disney's Saratoga Springs Resort and Spa at Walt Disney World?

54-6) 'The Legend of Johnny Appleseed', 'Little Toot' and 'Pecos Bill' were packaged together with other short segments to form which Disney film?

54-7) The metal toy soldiers who march in Disney's Christmas parades first appeared in which 1961 movie?

54-8) Who do Pain and Panic serve?

54-9) In what year did Disneyland move from A-E ticket books to a general admission ticket?

54-10) Who is Marcus Mouse?

Answers to Question Set 54

54-1) The yeti on the Matterhorn Bobsleds has the nickname Harold.

54-2) José Carioca appeared in 'Saludos Amigos' and 'The Three Caballeros'.

54-3) Milo and Nicky are friends of 'Pepper Ann' Pearson.

54-4) Jock and Trusty appeared in 'Lady and the Tramp'.

54-5) Disney's Saratoga Springs opened on the site of the old Disney Institute.

54-6) 'The Legend of Johnny Appleseed', 'Little Toot' and 'Pecos Bill' made up part of the movie 'Melody Time'.

54-7) The toy soldiers first appeared in 'Babes in Toyland'.

54-8) Pain and Panic are minions of Hades in the movie 'Hercules'.

54-9) A-E ticket books were finally phased out in June 1982.

54-10) Marcus Mouse, a farmer, is the father of Minnie Mouse.

Question Set 55

55-1) Which group of incompetent criminals are forever trying to steal Scrooge McDuck's fortune?

55-2) Which English town, after winning a competition in 2009, is now the twin town of Walt Disney World?

55-3) Which 1941 movie consists primarily of a tour of the Disney animation studios interspersed with four animated segment?

55-4) In which Walt Disney World attraction does the title character play a game of Jeopardy! against Jamie Lee Curtis and Albert Einstein?

55-5) What honour, America's highest civilian award, did Walt Disney receive from President Lyndon B. Johnson on September 14th 1964?

55-6) Which Disney's California Adventure ride closed within a year of opening despite including figures of Cher, Jackie Chan, Whoopi Goldberg, Cindy Crawford and others?

55-7) Whose major enemies were Fat Cat and Norton Nimnul?

55-8) What was the first movie to be released in Disney Digital 3-D?

55-9) Which service did Disney introduce in 2005 to transport visitors from Orlando International Airport to Walt Disney World?

55-10) What was the title of the feature length spin-off from the 'House of Mouse' TV series featuring Disney's bad guys?

Answers to Question Set 55

55-1) The Beagle Boys keep trying to steal from Uncle Scrooge.

55-2) Walt Disney World is twinned with the town of Swindon in England.

55-3) 'The Reluctant Dragon' features an extended tour of the Disney animation studios.

55-4) Ellen DeGeneres plays a game of Jeopardy! in Universe of Energy: Ellen's Energy Adventure.

55-5) President Lyndon B. Johnson awarded Walt Disney the Presidential Medal of Freedom.

55-6) The Superstar Limo ride at Disney's California Adventure was so unpopular that it was permanently closed down after just eleven months.

55-7) The Mafia-style grey tabby Fat Cat and mad scientist Norton Nimnul regularly went up against Chip 'n' Dale's Rescue Rangers.

55-8) The first Disney Digital 3-D movie was 'Chicken Little'.

55-9) Disney's Magical Express was introduced in 2005.

55-10) Disney's bad guys took over in 'Mickey's House of Villains'.

Question Set 56

56-1) Which Disney character's original name was Dippy Dawg?

56-2) 'Cory in the House' was a spin-off from which Disney TV series?

56-3) Who are Slightly, Nibs, Tootles, Curly and the Twins?

56-4) Where is Disney's Ambassador Hotel?

56-5) Which title character was played by Brendan Fraser in a live action Disney comedy, and Christopher Showerman in a straight-to-video sequel?

56-6) In which short film from 1938 does Mickey Mouse subdue a giant to win the fair Minnie's hand in marriage?

56-7) King Stefan and King Hubert are characters from which classic Disney movie?

56-8) Which show did Cirque du Soleil create for their base at Florida's Downtown Disney?

56-9) What is the name of the young garbage boy who befriends Remy in 'Ratatouille'?

56-10) What does Scrooge McDuck call the first coin that he ever earned?

Answers to Question Set 56

56-1) Goofy initially went under the name Dippy Dawg.

56-2) 'Cory in the House' was a spin-off from 'That's So Raven'.

56-3) Slightly, Nibs, Tootles, Curly and the Twins are 'Peter Pan's lost boys.

56-4) Guests can stay at Disney's Ambassador Hotel at Tokyo Disneyland.

56-5) Brendan Fraser and Christopher Showerman both played 'George of the Jungle'.

56-6) Mickey battles a giant in 1938's 'Brave Little Tailor'.

56-7) King Stefan and King Hubert appear in 'Sleeping Beauty'.

56-8) Downtown Disney is the only place to see Cirque du Soleil's 'La Nouba'.

56-9) Remy's young friend in 'Ratatouille' is called Alfredo Linguini.

56-10) Uncle Scrooge is particularly fond of his 'number one dime'.

Question Set 57

57-1) Which Disney character leads a double life as pop star 'Hannah Montana'?

57-2) EPCOT's The Land pavilion used to show a movie called 'Symbiosis'. What film shows in its place now?

57-3) Which Oscar-winning movie from 1948 was the first of Disney's True-Life Adventures?

57-4) The town of Rainbow Ridges (at Disneyland) and Tumbleweed (in the Magic Kingdom version) provide the backstory for which theme park ride?

57-5) What was the name of the lion raised by sheep in a 1951 Disney short?

57-6) Which magician put his name to a series of 'Magic Underground' restaurants? Despite a lot of publicity and the promise of opening at Disney's American theme parks, they never materialised.

57-7) In 2004 Mickey, Donald and Goofy starred as which trio of heroes in an adaptation of an Alexandre Dumas classic book?

57-8) In the 1977 live action movie starring Jodie Foster and David Niven, what is 'Candleshoe'?

57-9) Norbu, Bob, Serka, Norgay, Bhat, Ronin, Balram, Saint Yeti, Tibetan Warrior, Baichung, Tenzing and Spirit of Nepal are all vehicles on which Walt Disney World ride?

57-10) What is 4017 Disneya?

Answers to Question Set 57

57-1) Hannah Montana's alter ego is Miley Ray Stewart, played by Miley Cyrus.

57-2) In 1995, The Land pavilion at EPCOT replaced 'Symbiosis' with the more family friendly 'Circle of Life: An Environmental Fable'.

57-3) The first in the True-Life Adventure series was 'Seal Island'.

57-4) Rainbow Ridges and Tumbleweed are the fictional towns served by Big Thunder Mountain Railroad.

57-5) In 1951 Disney produced the Oscar nominated short movie 'Lambert the Sheepish Lion'.

57-6) Disney was to have housed some of David Copperfield's 'Magic Underground' restaurants.

57-7) Mickey, Donald and Goofy starred as 'The Three Musketeers'.

57-8) 'Candleshoe' was a large country house.

57-9) Norbu, Bob, Serka, Norgay, Bhat, Ronin, Balram, Saint Yeti, Tibetan Warrior, Baichung, Tenzing and Spirit of Nepal (along with Everest Explorer) are the ride vehicles on Expedition Everest.

57-10) 4017 Disneya is a minor planet orbiting our sun between Mars and Jupiter. It was discovered in February 1980 by Russian astronomers who named it in honour of Walt Disney.

Question Set 58

58-1) What is the name of Lightning McQueen's transporter truck in 'Cars'?

58-2) Who played Long John Silver in Disney's live action version of 'Treasure Island'?

58-3) What is the third, direct to video, instalment in the 'Honey I Shrunk the Kids' movie series?

58-4) Which musical leading man was the star of the adventure comedy, 'Condorman'.

58-5) Where can guests Meet The World while sitting in a revolving theatre?

58-6) Dick Van Dyke played a U.S. Navy pilot who becomes a castaway in which 1966 movie?

58-7) In 'Robin Hood', what kind of creature is Friar Tuck?

58-8) Where is Mount Gushmore?

58-9) Aladar, Yar and Plio are characters in which movie?

58-10) Which Disney online game allows a player's character to live in an igloo and keep Puffles as pets?

Answers to Question Set 58

58-1) Lightning McQueen's transporter is called Mack.

58-2) Robert Newton starred in 'Treasure Island' as Long John Silver.

58-3) The third film starring the Szalinski family was 'Honey, We Shrunk Ourselves'.

58-4) Michael Crawford starred as Woodrow (Woody) Wilkins AKA 'Condorman'.

58-5) Meet The World is in Tokyo Disneyland's Tomorrowland.

58-6) Dick van Dyke played the title role in 'Lt. Robin Crusoe, U.S.N.'

58-7) In 'Robin Hood', Andy Devine played Friar Tuck as an American badger.

58-8) Mount Gushmore is the main peak at Disney's Blizzard Beach waterpark.

58-9) Aladar, Yar and Plio all appear in 'Dinosaur'.

58-10) Puffles are pets in the Disney's Club Penguin franchise.

Question Set 59

59-1) Which 1975 live action movie sees an Apatosaurus skeleton stolen from London's Natural History Museum?

59-2) Walt Disney holds the record for receiving the most Oscar awards. How many did he win?

59-3) What was the name of the malamute who was a 'Wild Dog of the North' according to the title of a 1961 Disney live action film?

59-4) What was the gondola lift attraction that travelled between Disneyland's Fantasyland and Tomorrowland called?

59-5) Who, apart from the Emperor Kuzco, has been the star of his own 'New Groove' movie?

59-6) What is Thomas O'Malley's full name in 'The Aristocats'?

59-7) Who is Duckburg's most famous inventor?

59-8) From where were the famous Lipizzaner dancing horses evacuated in 1963's 'Miracle of the White Stallions'?

59-9) Which film from 1961 is based on the apparently true story of a Skye Terrier who became a tourist attraction when he slept every night on his late owner's grave in Edinburgh?

59-10) What is the only Disney ride to offer motion sickness bags to riders?

Answers to Question Set 59

59-1) The Apatosaurus skeleton was stolen in 'One of Our Dinosaurs is Missing'.

59-2) Walt won 22 Oscars (including one posthumously) and was also awarded four honorary Oscars. Many of them are on display at the Walt Disney Family Museum in San Francisco.

59-3) The malamute dog in Disney's 1961 movie was 'Nikki, Wild Dog of the North'.

59-4) Disneyland's gondola lift was called the Skyway.

59-5) 'The Emperor's New Groove' was followed by a sequel, 'Kronk's New Groove'.

59-6) The alley cat's full name is Abraham de Lacy Giuseppe Casey Thomas O'Malley.

59-7) The chicken Gyro Gearloose is the most celebrated inventor in Duckburg.

59-8) The Lipizzaner white stallions were evacuated from the Spanish Riding School in Vienna, Austria, during World War II.

59-9) The Skye Terrier was called 'Greyfriars Bobby'.

59-10) Motion sickness bags have been supplied on EPCOT's Mission: Space ride.

Question Set 60

60-1) In 'The Hunchback of Notre Dame', what falls on the sixth of January?

60-2) Who directed 'Captain EO', the Michael Jackson 3D movie?

60-3) Which former EPCOT ride shared a similar storyline to the classic sci-fi movie 'Fantastic Voyage'?

60-4) Which 2007 novel by Mark Peter Hughes, about a group of high school teenagers who meet in detention and form a rock band, was made into a Disney TV movie?

60-5) Which city does Herbie race towards in the third Love Bug movie?

60-6) In a Disney short movie, which bull was taken to fight in the bullring in Madrid, even though all he wanted to do was smell flowers all day?

60-7) Dean Jones inherited a run-down hotel in a Colorado ski village in which 1972 Disney comedy?

60-8) 'Tangled' was originally to have been given which title?

60-9) In which year did Walt Disney World host its first official 'Star Wars' weekend?

60-10) What is Princess Jasmine's tiger called in 'Aladdin'?

Answers to Question Set 60

60-1) The sixth of January is Topsy Turvy day, the Feast of Fools.

60-2) 'Captain EO' was directed by Hollywood legend Francis Ford Coppola.

60-3) EPCOT's Body Wars reminded many guests of 'Fantastic Voyage'.

60-4) Mark Peter Hughes wrote 'Lemonade Mouth'.

60-5) The third Love Bug movie was 'Herbie Goes to Monte Carlo'.

60-6) 'Ferdinand the Bull' loved flowers, not fighting.

60-7) Dean Jones inherited the Grand Imperial Hotel in 'Snowball Express'.

60-8) 'Tangled' was initially known as 'Rapunzel Unbraided' and then simply 'Rapunzel'.

60-9) 'Star Wars' weekends began at the Disney-MGM Studios park in 1997.

60-10) Princess Jasmine's tiger is called Rajah.

Question Set 61

61-1) Where can guests dine in a restaurant named Remy?

61-2) Donald Duck had a nightmare of working in a Nazi munitions factory in which famous wartime propaganda movie?

61-3) What was celebrated by the Happiest Homecoming on Earth?

61-4) Which live action comedy-drama from 1995 showed a U.S. plan to secretly transport a full-grown elephant across 200 miles of rugged terrain during the war in Vietnam?

61-5) Name the three stuffed animal heads that introduce The Country Bear Jamboree at the Magic Kingdom.

61-6) What is the name of Rapunzel's pet chameleon in 'Tangled'?

61-7) Paul Newman's final major movie role was as the voice of which character?

61-8) In what year was pin trading officially introduced to Walt Disney World?

61-9) What was the 2002 animated sequel to 'Peter Pan' called?

61-10) Which 1953 live action movie tells the story of young Mary Tudor, sister of England's King Henry VIII?

Answers to Question Set 61

61-1) Remy is a 'Ratatouille'-themed restaurant on board the Disney Dream cruise ship.

61-2) Donald Duck threw a tomato at Adolf Hitler in 'Der Fuehrer's Face'.

61-3) Starting in May 2005, the Happiest Homecoming on Earth was an 18 month celebration of 50 years of Disney theme parks.

61-4) An elephant flew (albeit via a parachute) in 'Operation Dumbo Drop'.

61-5) The trophy heads in The Country Bear Jamboree are Buff (a bison), Max (a stag) and Melvin (a moose).

61-6) Rapunzel's pet chameleon is called Pascal.

61-7) Paul Newman voiced Doc Hudson in 'Cars'.

61-8) Cast members began trading pins at Walt Disney World in 1999 as part of the Millennium Celebration.

61-9) 'Peter Pan 2' was subtitled 'Return to Never Land'.

61-10) Mary Tudor's story was told in 'The Sword and The Rose'.

Question Set 62

62-1) A young boy named Cody is captured in an Australian animal trap in which animated movie?

62-2) What is the English pub at EPCOT called?

62-3) Who is the English bad guy in 'Pocahontas'?

62-4) ...and what kind of dog does he have?

62-5) What is the name of the orphaned 'Lonesome Cougar' who is raised by humans before being successfully released into the wild in a 1967 Disney live action movie?

62-6) Which evil character is voiced by Kelsey Grammar in 'Toy Story 2'?

62-7) What kind of animal was the star of the animated TV series 'Bonkers'?

62-8) Where is Disney's award-winning Napa Rose restaurant?

62-9) Mickey Mouse made a guest appearance in which Jimmy Durante musical?

62-10) Who does 'WALL-E' fall in love with?

Answers to Question Set 62

62-1) Cody appears in 'The Rescuers Down Under'.

62-2) EPCOT's English pub is The Rose and Crown.

62-3) In 'Pocahontas', Governor Ratcliffe is the main villain.

62-4) Ratcliffe has a pet Pug called Percy.

62-5) Disney released 'Charlie, the Lonesome Cougar' in 1967.

62-6) Kelsey Grammar played Stinky Pete the Prospector in 'Toy Story 2'.

62-7) The star of 'Bonkers' was Bonkers D. Bobcat.

62-8) The Napa Rose restaurant is in the Grand Californian hotel at Disneyland.

62-9) Mickey Mouse appeared in Jimmy Durante's 'Hollywood Party' in 1934.

62-10) 'WALL-E' falls in love with the **E**xtraterrestrial **V**egetation **E**valuator, EVE.

Question Set 63

63-1) In 'The Sword in the Stone', what is Merlin's pet owl called?

63-2) Minnie Mouse created which teddy bear for Mickey to take with him on a long sea voyage?

63-3) In 'The Nightmare Before Christmas', what is the name of Jack Skellington's dog?

63-4) Whose crew include Fuzzball, Idey and Ody, Major Domo and Minor Domo, and Hooter.

63-5) A shape-shifting pink blob named Morph appears in which Disney animated movie?

63-6) In which animated movie did Vincent Price provide the voice of the evil Professor Ratigan?

63-7) Comedienne and talk-show host Rosie O'Donnell voiced which character in 'Tarzan'?

63-8) Dave Smith was founder and head of which Disney division for forty years?

63-9) Which boat ride was replaced by the Gran Fiesta Tour starring The Three Caballeros in EPCOT's Mexico pavilion?

63-10) Which short Pixar film about a magician with an uncooperative rabbit was shown in movie theatres alongside 'WALL-E'?

Answers to Question Set 63

63-1) Merlin's owl is called Archimedes.

63-2) Mickey's teddy is Duffy the Disney bear. He's so named because Mickey found him hidden in his duffel bag.

63-3) Jack Skellington owns a ghost dog called Zero.

63-4) They are 'Captain EO's crew.

63-5) Morph appeared in 'Treasure Planet'.

63-6) Vincent Price voiced Professor Ratigan in 'The Great Mouse Detective'.

63-7) Rosie O'Donnell played the voice of Terk in 'Tarzan'.

63-8) Dave Smith founded the Disney Archives in 1970 and was chief archivist until his retirement in 2010.

63-9) The Gran Fiesta Tour replaced El Rio del Tiempo, The River of Time.

63-10) 'Presto' was shown in cinemas before 'WALL-E'.

Question Set 64

64-1) Which Tim Burton Disney musical, starring Paul Terry as the title character, begins as a live action movie before switching to stop-motion, and later combines the two film formats?

64-2) In 'Fantasia', who are Brudus and Melinda?

64-3) Which two boys lived on the Triple R Ranch in three 'Mickey Mouse Club' serials in the 1950's?

64-4) Randy Quaid voiced which antagonist in 'Home on the Range'?

64-5) Who is The Barbarian in the title of a Disney animated TV series?

64-6) Which full length animated movie helped to convince Franklin D. Roosevelt to commit to a strategy of long-range bombing during World War II?

64-7) Which Pixar movie was originally to be titled 'The Bear and the Bow'?

64-8) In which classic animated movie do the characters Flaps, Buzzie, Dizzy and Ziggy appear?

64-9) Where could you dine at Hook's Pointe?

64-10) Which Mickey Mouse short film was the last programme shown by the BBC in England before they closed services for the duration of World War II?

Answers to Question Set 64

64-1) Paul Terry played the title role in 'James and the Giant Peach'.

64-2) Brudus and Melinda are the blue-skinned centaur lovers in 'Fantasia', although their names are never mentioned in the movie.

64-3) 'Spin and Marty' lived on the Triple R Ranch.

64-4) Randy Quaid plays the voice of Alameda Slim.

64-5) Disney produced 'Dave The Barbarian' in 2004.

64-6) President Roosevelt was impressed by Disney's propaganda movie, 'Victory Through Air Power'.

64-7) 'The Bear and the Bow' was the working title of 'Brave'.

64-8) Flaps, Buzzie, Dizzy and Ziggy are the vultures in 'The Jungle Book' who look and sound uncannily like The Beatles.

64-9) Hook's Pointe was a restaurant at the Disneyland Hotel in California.

64-10) The BBC ceased transmission on September 1st 1939, in the middle of 'Mickey's Gala Premiere'. So it was only fitting that when they resumed broadcasting after the war on June 7th 1946, this cartoon was shown in its entirety.

Question Set 65

65-1) In the 'High School Musical' movies, Ryan Evans is the twin brother of which other character?

65-2) Which Disney actress had hit singles with the songs Tall Paul, First Name Initial, O Dio Mio, and Train of Love?

65-3) Luigi's Flying Tyres at Disney's California Adventure's Cars Land is an updated version of which early Disneyland attraction?

65-4) What was the first computer generated short film to win an Academy Award?

65-5) Which Disney animated movie went under the working title of 'Kingdom of the Sun'?

65-6) What role did Scatman Crothers voice in 'The Aristocats'?

65-7) What momentous speech was given at the ballroom of the at Disney's Contemporary on November 17th 1973?

65-8) Who famously said that Disneyland Paris was 'not my cup of tea'?

65-9) What was the subtitle of the straight-to-video sequel to 'Pocahontas'?

65-10) Dr Calico is the bad guy in which CGI movie?

Answers to Question Set 65

65-1) Sharpay Evans is Ryan's twin sister.

65-2) The singing actress was Annette Funicello.

65-3) Luigi's Flying Tyres is a modern version of Disneyland's Flying Saucers hovercraft ride.

65-4) Pixar's 'Tin Toy' was the company's first Oscar when it won the award for Best Animated Short in 1989.

65-5) 'Kingdom of the Sun' was eventually released as 'The Emperor's New Groove'.

65-6) Scatman Crothers was the unforgettable Scat Cat.

65-7) On November 17th 1973 American President Richard M. Nixon told reporters assembled in the Contemporary's ballroom, 'I am not a crook'.

65-8) The late French President François Mitterrand did not care for Disneyland Paris.

65-9) The sequel to 'Pocahontas' was 'Pocahontas II: Voyage to a New World'.

65-10) 'Bolt's nemesis is Dr Calico.

Question Set 66

66-1) In 'Monsters Inc.' what item of clothing does the monster George Sanderson have stuck to his back?

66-2) The 1955 movie 'The Littlest Outlaw' was set in which country?

66-3) Which Disney theme park features an area called World Bazaar?

66-4) 'The Light in the Forest', 'Davy Crockett, King of the Wild Frontier', 'Davy Crockett and the River Pirates' and 'Johnny Tremain' were given what collective title when released to video in 1997?

66-5) In which True Life Adventure film does a female squirrel meet up with a male, Porro?

66-6) What are the names of Lady's owners in 'Lady and the Tramp'?

66-7) What animal is 'Tonka', the title role in a 1958 Disney live action movie?

66-8) Who wrote and performed songs for Pixar's 'A Bug's Life', 'Monsters, Inc.', 'Cars' and 'Toy Story' movies?

66-9) Which short-lived section of Disneyland featured a circus and a baseball diamond?

66-10) Which two characters feature on the Mobile Muppet Lab roving theme park animatronic?

Answers to Question Set 66

66-1) George finds a child's sock on his back.

66-2) 'The Littlest Outlaw' is about a boy who runs away with a General's horse that has been cruelly treated in Mexico.

66-3) World Bazaar is the glass-covered equivalent of Main Street U.S.A. at Tokyo Disneyland.

66-4) 'The Light in the Forest', 'Davy Crockett, King of the Wild Frontier', 'Davy Crockett and the River Pirates' and 'Johnny Tremain' were collectively 'The Great American Legends' series.

66-5) In 'Perri' the female squirrel finds her mate, Porro.

66-6) The couple that Lady lives with are only referred ever to as Jim Dear and Darling although early versions of the script called them Jim Brown and his wife, Elizabeth.

66-7) 'Tonka' is a horse that was ridden in the Battle of Little Big Horn.

66-8) Randy Newman wrote songs for many Pixar movies.

66-9) Holidayland opened at Disneyland in 1957, but closed just four years later.

66-10) Dr Bunsen Honeydew and Beaker ride on the Mobile Muppet Lab.

Question Set 67

67-1) Which song from 'Bambi' was nominated for the 1942 Best Original Song Academy Award?

67-2) What is the name of the Huntsman that the Wicked Queen sends to kill Snow White?

67-3) Actors Kathryn Beaumont, Bill Thompson and Heather Angel worked together on which two classic Disney animations?

67-4) What was the title creature in 'Rascal'?

67-5) What is the name of the lamp that forms the 'i' in the Pixar logo?

67-6) Which Disney stage musical follows the recording of a Disney's greatest hits album in a magical recording studio?

67-7) Which Disney Channel TV series is based around a nurse and an exterminator trying to come to terms with the birth of their fourth child, Charlotte?

67-8) What job did Lillian Bounds do before she married Walt Disney?

67-9) 'Bumble Boogie' and 'Blame it on the Samba' are segments from which Disney animated movie?

67-10) In which 1964 Disney movie (based on a Mary Stewart suspense novel) did Hayley Mills try to foil a jewel thief on the island of Crete?

Answers to Question Set 67

67-1) While Little April Shower is probably 'Bambi's best-remembered song, Love is a Song was nominated for the Oscar, though the winner that year was White Christmas.

67-2) Although never named in 'Snow White and the Seven Dwarfs', promotional material gives the Huntsman's name as Humbert.

67-3) Kathryn Beaumont voiced Alice in 'Alice in Wonderland' and Wendy in 'Peter Pan'. Bill Thompson was the White Rabbit and Mr Smee, while Heather Angel played Alice's sister and Wendy's mother, Mary Darling.

67-4) 'Rascal' was a pet raccoon in a 1969 live action movie.

67-5) Pixar's lamp is called Luxo jr. He was the title star of the company's first film in 1986.

67-6) The stage musical 'On the Record' celebrates 75 years of Disney music.

67-7) Charlotte is the baby in 'Good Luck Charlie'.

67-8) Lillian Bounds was an ink artist at the Disney Studio before she married the boss.

67-9) 'Bumble Boogie' and 'Blame it on the Samba' are sequences from 1948's 'Melody Time'.

67-10) Hayley Mills came up against Eli Wallach's jewel thief in 'The Moon-Spinners'.

Question Set 68

68-1) Which live action movie (with a large animated character) is set in the fictional Maine town of Passamaquoddy?

68-2) 'The Resurrection of Doom' was a graphic novel sequel to which movie?

68-3) Disney's first timeshare resort, The Disney Vacation Club Resort at Walt Disney World, now goes under what name?

68-4) The cancellation of which movie lead to the closure of the Orlando arm of Disney's animation studio?

68-5) Which 1983 live action Disney (yet very un-Disney-like) movie was based upon a novel by Ray Bradbury and featured a carnival proprietor offering to fulfil people's wildest dreams?

68-6) Queen Leah is the mother of which Disney Princess, although her name is never mentioned onscreen?

68-7) Which Disney stage show includes the song Brimstone and Treacle?

68-8) What was the first Disney animated movie to be given a PG (parental guidance suggested) rating by the Motion Picture Association of America?

68-9) What is Golden Oak in California, purchased by Walt Disney in 1959?

68-10) What is Golden Oak, which opened at Walt Disney World in 2011?

Answers to Question Set 68

68-1) 'Pete's Dragon' is set in Passamaquoddy.

68-2) 'The Resurrection of Doom' followed the events of 'Who Framed Roger Rabbit?'

68-3) The Disney Vacation Club Resort is now known as Disney's Old Key West Resort.

68-4) Disney's animation studio at the MGM Studios theme park closed shortly after they pulled the plug on a movie that started out as 'The Ghost and his Gift' and at various times had gone through the names 'A Few Good Ghosts', 'My Peoples', 'Angel and Her No Good Sister', 'Elgin's People' and 'Once in a Blue Moon'.

68-5) Ray Bradbury wrote the script for the movie based upon his own novel, 'Something Wicked This Way Comes'.

68-6) Queen Leah is the mother of Aurora, the 'Sleeping Beauty'.

68-7) The song Brimstone and Treacle appears in the 'Mary Poppins' stage show when another nanny gives the children her own, less palatable version of a spoonful of sugar.

68-8) In 1985 'The Black Cauldron' became the first Disney animated movie to be rated PG due to a few quite violent scenes.

68-9) Walt Disney bought the Golden Oak Ranch in California as a site for filming 'old west' scenes without visible intrusion of modern buildings and roads.

68-10) Golden Oak is Walt Disney World's exclusive luxury residential community.

Question Set 69

69-1) In which classic short film featuring Mickey, Donald and Goofy does Donald Duck sing Hickory Dickory Dock?

69-2) Where is the Hotel MiraCosta?

69-3) Which creature is the mascot of Disney's Blizzard Beach water park?

69-4) Which character regularly played a gossip columnist (with the catchphrase 'gossip is always true!') in 'Disney's House of Mouse'?

69-5) In the 'Pirates of the Caribbean' movies, Will Turner's father is also called William. But what is his nickname?

69-6) Which body-swap comedy movie has Disney made three times?

69-7) What is the Disney Vacation Club expansion to Disney's Animal Kingdom Lodge called?

69-8) Which animated movie features the song Oh Sing, Sweet Nightingale?

69-9) Where was the True Life Adventure short film 'Nature's Half Acre' set?

69-10) Madame Medusa is the main villain in which animated movie?

Answers to Question Set 69

69-1) Donald sings Hickory Dickory Dock in 'The Clock Cleaners'.

69-2) The Hotel MiraCosta is located above the Mediterranean Harbor port at Tokyo DisneySea.

69-3) An alligator called Ice Gator is Blizzard Beach's mascot. He occasionally made public appearances during the water park's early days. Typhoon Lagoon's mascot is Lagoona Gator.

69-4) Clarabelle Cow had a regular role in 'Disney's House of Mouse' as a gossip columnist.

69-5) Will Turner's dad is nicknamed Bootstrap Bill.

69-6) There have been three versions of 'Freaky Friday'. Jodie Foster starred in the original 1976 release. Then came a TV movie version in 1995, and most recently Lindsay Lohan and Jamie Lee Curtis swapped bodies for a 2003 remake.

69-7) The expansion to Disney's Animal Kingdom Lodge is called Kidani Village. The original Lodge building was renamed Jambo House.

69-8) Oh Sing, Sweet Nightingale is in 'Cinderella'.

69-9) 'Nature's Half Acre' showed the natural changes in a typical American meadow throughout the four seasons.

69-10) Madame Medusa appears in 'The Rescuers'. The snake-headed Medusa of Greek mythology made an appearance in the 'Hercules' cartoon series, where she was voiced by Jennifer Love Hewitt.

Question Set 70

70-1) In a direct-to-video sequel, French Stewart replaced Matthew Broderick as John Brown, the alter-ego of which hero?

70-2) Which part live action / part animated movie features the songs Sooner or Later, All I Want, Let the Rain Pour Down and Who Wants to Live Like That?

70-3) Where has Disney announced they will build Grizzly Trail?

70-4) What is the Evil Queen from 'Snow White' actually called?

70-5) 'Off His Rockers', an early computer animated movie about a rocking horse whose owner would rather play video games than ride him, was originally released to cinemas alongside which 1992 Disney live action movie?

70-6) Walt Disney made his early 'Laugh-O-Gram' films for which cinema chain?

70-7) The Midway Mania! theme park attraction is based upon which movie?

70-8) The name of the 'It's Tough to be a Bug!' attraction was inspired by which 1969 short film?

70-9) Billy Hill and the Hillbillies regularly play at which venue?

70-10) Which Disney character got drafted into the army in a 1942 short film?

Answers to Question Set 70

70-1) French Stewart and Matthew Broderick played John Brown AKA 'Inspector Gadget'.

70-2) Sooner or Later, All I Want, Let the Rain Pour Down and Who Wants to Live Like That? all feature in 'Song of the South'.

70-3) Grizzly Trail is being created as an expansion at Hong Kong Disneyland.

70-4) In early 'Snow White' publicity material the Evil Witch's name was given as Queen Grimhilde.

70-5) 'Off His Rockers' was the theatrical opener for 'Honey, I Blew Up the Kid'.

70-6) The series of films were officially titled 'Newman's Laugh-O-Grams' after the Newman cinemas that commissioned them.

70-7) The theme park shooting attraction's full name is Toy Story Midway Mania!

70-8) Disney released the short 'It's Tough to be a Bird' in 1969.

70-9) Billy Hill and the Hillbillies play at the Golden Horseshoe Saloon in Disneyland.

70-10) Donald Duck joined the army in the short propaganda film 'Donald Gets Drafted'.

Question Set 71

71-1) Which Disney nature documentary allegedly gave birth to the urban myth about lemming suicides?

71-2) What 1935 short, which made heavy use of Rossini's William Tell Overture in its soundtrack, was the first Mickey Mouse film produced in colour?

71-3) French electronic music duo Daft Punk recorded the soundtrack for, and briefly appeared in, which Disney sequel?

71-4) In which short film did Pluto make his first appearance without Mickey Mouse?

71-5) Dean Jones starred in which 1966 movie about a Great Dane who thought he was a different kind of dog?

71-6) Billy Campbell played stunt pilot Cliff Secord in which Disney superhero movie?

71-7) What is 'Handy Manny's surname?

71-8) The Disney Village shopping and dining area at Disneyland Paris originally went under which other name?

71-9) Helen Silbert, Dessie Flynn (AKA Dessie Miller), James MacDonald, Tress MacNeille and Corey Burton have all provided voices for which Disney comedy duo?

71-10) Christopher Robin was replaced by which female character as the lead human in the TV series 'My Friends Tigger and Pooh'?

Answers to Question Set 71

71-1) A scene from the film 'White Wilderness' showing lemmings supposedly leaping into the Arctic Ocean is believed to have been the start of the myth that lemmings commit suicide.

71-2) The first Mickey Mouse film to be made in colour was 'The Band Concert'.

71-3) Daft Punk composed the score for 'Tron: Legacy'. They can be seen in the movie as DJs in Castor's The End of the Line nightclub.

71-4) Pluto's first solo movie was the 1932 Silly Symphony 'Just Dogs'.

71-5) The Great Dane believed that he was 'The Ugly Dachshund'.

71-6) Cliff Secord was 'The Rocketeer'.

71-7) Manuel Garcia is the main character in the TV series 'Handy Manny'.

71-8) When Euro Disney opened in 1992 its shopping and dining was called Festival Disney.

71-9) Helen Silbert, Dessie Flynn, James MacDonald, Tress MacNeille and Corey Burton have all provided voices for Chip an' Dale.

71-10) The tomboy girl in 'My Friends Tigger and Pooh' was called Darby.

Question Set 72

72-1) Released under the Touchstone Films imprint in 1986, what was the first Disney movie to carry an 'R' (for 'restricted') rating in the USA?

72-2) Which Disney channel TV series used the song Everything is Not What it Seems as its theme tune?

72-3) Which animated movie adapted music from a Tchaikovsky ballet for its soundtrack?

72-4) In the 1988 television special 'Totally Minnie', Minnie Mouse sings a duet with which British knight?

72-5) How many brothers and sisters did Walt Disney have?

72-6) Which animated movie features the mouse Roquefort?

72-7) What was the name of the parade that preceded Illuminations: Reflections of Earth in EPCOT's Millennium Celebration?

72-8) What 2004 part live action / part animated short movie featuring Julie Andrews is based on part of the book 'Mary Poppins Opens the Door'?

72-9) What Tim Rice & Alan Menken musical was the opening production at Disney's renovated New Amsterdam Theatre in New York?

72-10) In the late 1930's Hemlock Peak in the Californian Sugar Bowl ski resort was renamed what?

Answers to Question Set 72

72-1) Disney's first 'R' rated movie was 'Down and Out in Beverley Hills'.

72-2) Selena Gomez sang Everything is Not What it Seems over the credits of 'Wizards of Waverley Place'.

72-3) Much of 'Sleeping Beauty's soundtrack was adapted from Tchaikovsky's ballet of the same name.

72-4) Minnie sang Don't Go Breakin' My Heart with Sir Elton John.

72-5) Walt had one younger sister (Ruth) and three older brothers (Herbert, Raymond and Roy).

72-6) Roquefort is a helpful mouse in 'The Aristocats'.

72-7) Each night EPCOT's Illuminations: Reflections of Earth show was preceded by the Tapestry of Nations parade.

72-8) 'Mary Poppins Opens the Door' formed the basis of the short 'The Cat That Looked at a King'.

72-9) Tim Rice & Alan Menken's 'King David' musical was chosen as the opening show at the New Amsterdam Theatre.

72-10) Hemlock Peak was renamed Mount Disney.

Question Set 73

73-1) What was the name of the Disney theme park that was proposed for St Louis, Missouri in the mid-1960s?

73-2) Which singer and actress is the official Godmother of the Disney Dream cruise ship?

73-3) What was the title of the direct-to-video sequel to 'Hercules'?

73-4) What does Goofy call his superhero alter-ego?

73-5) Ving Rhames provided the voice for which character in 'Lilo and Stitch'?

73-6) Who took over as chairman, CEO, and president of the Walt Disney Company on Walt's death in 1966?

73-7) On 31 December 2009 Disney acquired which comic book company for a reported $4.24 billion?

73-8) What was the first film that Robert and Richard Sherman worked on as Disney staff songwriters?

73-9) What was the Magic Kingdom's Tomorrowland Transit Authority PeopleMover previously known as?

73-10) Which live action movie featured the robots Vital Information Necessary CENTralized and BiO-sanitation Battalion?

Answers to Question Set 73

73-1) Had Disney's St Louis, Missouri theme park gone ahead it would have been called Walt Disney's Riverfront Square.

73-2) Jennifer Hudson is the Disney Dream's official Godmother. She worked as a singer for the cruise line before she found fame on American Idol.

73-3) 'Hercules: Zero to Hero' was released direct to video. It shared much of its material with the 'Hercules' animated TV series.

73-4) When Goofy eats Super Goobers he becomes the costumed hero Super Goof.

73-5) Ving Rhames provided the voice of the former CIA Agent Cobra Bubbles.

73-6) After Walt Disney died his brother Roy took over the running of the company.

73-7) On the last day of 2009 Disney bought Marvel Entertainment Inc.

73-8) Robert and Richard Sherman's first movie for Disney was 1962's Oscar-nominated featurette 'A Symposium on Popular Songs'.

73-9) The Tomorrowland Transit Authority PeopleMover was previously known as the WEDway PeopleMover.

73-10) The robots Vital Information Necessary CENTralized and BiO-sanitation Battalion (better known as VINCENT and Old BOB) appeared in 'The Black Hole'.

Question Set 74

74-1) Which indoor Disney attraction opened in Chicago in 1999 but closed just two years later due to low attendance figures?

74-2) What is the train called that transports the circus in 'Dumbo'?

74-3) What was the most expensive movie of any released in 2000?

74-4) What did Mickey and the PhilharMagic Orchestra replace in the Fantasyland Concert Hall at the Magic Kingdom?

74-5) Which short film was shown in cinemas with 'Up' and also appeared on its DVD release?

74-6) What are the three gargoyles called in 'The Hunchback of Notre Dame'?

74-7) What appeared for the first time on January 13th 1930?

74-8) Debbie Ryan plays a Texas nanny to four children in which Disney Channel sitcom?

74-9) Who is the evil puppet maker in 'Pinocchio'?

74-10) Which Christmas movie tells the story of a boy selling his beloved old donkey to a carpenter who needs it to transport his pregnant wife to Bethlehem?

Answers to Question Set 74

74-1) Chicago housed the first DisneyQuest outside of Walt Disney World. Had it been a success it would have launched a series of similar indoor theme parks throughout America.

74-2) The train in 'Dumbo' is called Casey Junior.

74-3) With an official budget of $130 million, 'Dinosaur' was the most expensive movie released in 2000.

74-4) PhilharMagic replaced The Legend of the Lion King, a stage show featuring costumed characters and puppets, which ran from 1994 to 2002 at the Magic Kingdom. A different, Broadway-style show also titled The Legend of the Lion King ran for a while at Disneyland Paris.

74-5) 'Up' was supported by 'Partly Cloudy'.

74-6) The gargoyles on the cathedral of Notre Dame are called Victor, Hugo, and Laverne.

74-7) On January 13th 1930 Mickey Mouse appeared in a daily newspaper comic strip for the first time.

74-8) Debbie Ryan plays 'Jessie'.

74-9) The villainous puppeteer in 'Pinocchio' is called Stromboli.

74-10) Disney's much-loved Christmas short movie is called 'The Small One'.

Question Set 75

75-1) In 'Alice in Wonderland', what is Alice's cat called?

75-2) In what short cartoon did Chip and Dale first appear?

75-3) Future Hobbit Elijah Wood starred as the title character in which 1993 adaptation of a Mark Twain novel?

75-4) Bell, AT&T and Siemens have been among the sponsors for which EPCOT attraction?

75-5) In which Disney movie does Dwayne 'The Rock' Johnson play an American football quarterback who is forced to look after his eight-year-old daughter?

75-6) Which 1967 Dean Jones movie featured the last screen appearance of French actor and singer Maurice Chevalier?

75-7) What was the official greeting (and the signature cocktail) of the Adventurers Club at Pleasure Island?

75-8) Basil Rathbone, one of cinema's most acclaimed Sherlock Holmes actors, was the narrator of which classic Disney animation?

75-9) 'The Streets' was the second film in which Touchstone dance series?

75-10) What are the 'orphans' in the 1931 short film 'Mickey's Orphans'?

Answers to Question Set 75

75-1) Alice's cat is called Dinah.

75-2) Disney's mischievous duo first appeared in 1943's 'Private Pluto' although they appeared as unnamed, generic chipmunks in that. It wasn't until 'Chip an' Dale' in 1947 that they gained their full personalities and names.

75-3) Elijah Wood starred in 'The Adventures of Huck Finn'.

75-4) Bell, AT&T and Siemens have all sponsored Spaceship Earth.

75-5) The Rock played Boston Rebels quarterback Joe Kingman in 2007's 'The Game Plan'.

75-6) Maurice Chevalier's final movie was the comedy 'Monkeys, Go Home'.

75-7) Members of the Adventurers Club greet each other with a cry of 'Kungaloosh!'

75-8) Basil Rathbone narrated 'The Wind in the Willows', the Toad of Toad Hall segment of 1949's 'The Adventures of Ichabod and Mr Toad'.

75-9) The second 'Step Up' movie was titled 'Step Up 2: The Streets'.

75-10) 'Mickey's Orphans' are a bagful of abandoned kittens that Mickey and Minnie take into their home.

Question Set 76

76-1) Which 1964 family drama featured a Bengal tiger escaping a traveling circus and causing panic in a small town? It was also the great Indian actor Sabu's final movie.

76-2) Where is the world's largest outdoor wave pool?

76-3) Which planned expansion of Disney's Animal Kingdom would have focussed on dragons, unicorns and other mythical creatures?

76-4) James Garner rode what strange mode of transport in the 1973 Western movie 'One Little Indian'?

76-5) To which scouting organisation do Huey, Dewey and Louie belong?

76-6) Disney Legends Jodi Benson and Paige O'Hara have both provided the voice for which Disney character?

76-7) Which live action comedy starring Margot Kidder as a mystery writer who cracks an international plutonium smuggling ring was described by critics Siskel and Ebert as one of the Worst Films of 1983?

76-8) Which attraction at Disney's Hollywood Studios starred Drew Carey in a pilot for a fictitious TV show called 'Undercover Live'?

76-9) Clarence 'Ducky' Nash created Donald Duck's voice for Donald's first film in 1934 and continued to voice the duck for over 50 years. What was the last film for which Nash spoke as Donald?

76-10) At which theme park does Disney hold an annual International Food and Wine Festival and an International Flower and Garden Festival?

Answers to Question Set 76

76-1) Sabu's last film was 'A Tiger Walks'.

76-2) The world's largest outdoor wave pool is at Walt Disney World's Typhoon Lagoon.

76-3) The planned expansion of Disney's Animal Kingdom was to have been called the Beastly Kingdom. The Camp Minnie Mickey meet and greet area fills part of the area where the Beastly Kingdom would have been located.

76-4) In 'One Little Indian' James Garner played a camel-riding infantryman.

76-5) Huey, Dewey and Louie are Junior Woodchucks.

76-6) Paige O'Hara was the voice of Belle in 'Beauty and the Beast' and its sequels, but Jodi Benson was called in to provide Belle's voice for her appearances in the 'House of Mouse' TV series.

76-7) Margot Kidder's 'Trenchcoat' was a box office flop.

76-8) Drew Carey was the star of Sounds Dangerous!

76-9) Clarence Nash's final film as the voice of Donald was 'Mickey's Christmas Carol' in 1983, though he continued to provide the Duck's voice for Disney promotional work right up to his death two years later.

76-10) The International Food and Wine Festival and the International Flower and Garden Festival are both held annually at EPCOT.

Question Set 77

77-1) Which animation movie, which was originally to be called 'Sweating Bullets', did Disney announce was to be their final film to use any traditional hand drawing techniques?

77-2) Patrick Stewart plays the sheep language teacher Mr Woolensworth in which movie?

77-3) Where can you see a live magic show where the actors interact with a 3D movie of the Genie from Aladdin?

77-4) The villainous Don Karnage was commander of The Iron Vulture in which animated TV series?

77-5) Work on Pixar's film 'Newt' was halted when it was noted that it was very similar to which 20th Century Fox animated movie?

77-6) Which evil animated character does Fidget the Bat work for?

77-7) At Hong Kong Disneyland, what is Inspiration Lake?

77-8) In 'The Princess and the Frog', which frog does Princess Tiana fall in love with?

77-9) What was the name of the Disney videogame that starts with the final scene of 'The Incredibles' movie?

77-10) 'Hawaiian Vacation' was the first in a series of short films based on which animated franchise?

Answers to Question Set 77

77-1) 'Sweating Bullets' was eventually released as 'Home on the Range'. Although Disney said it was to be their final movie to use any traditional hand drawing techniques, this decision was later reversed when 'The Princess and the Frog' went into production.

77-2) Mr Woolensworth appears in 'Chicken Little'.

77-3) The Genie is the star of The Magic Lamp Theater at Tokyo DisneySea.

77-4) Don Karnage and his Air Pirates were the main bad guys in 'TaleSpin'.

77-5) Pixar's 'Newt' was very similar to Fox's 'Rio'.

77-6) Fidget the Bat is initially the henchman of Professor Padraic Ratigan in 'The Great Mouse Detective', but he later reforms.

77-7) Hong Kong Disneyland's Inspiration Lake is a tranquil recreation area just outside the park where guests can hire boats and surrey bikes. It's the largest man-made lake in Hong Kong and also serves as the park's irrigation reservoir.

77-8) Princess Tiana marries Prince Naveen of Maldonia.

77-9) 'The Incredibles: Rise of the Underminer' continues the story at the end of the movie.

77-10) 'Hawaiian Vacation' was the first in the Toy Story Toons series.

Question Set 78

78-1) Patrick McGoohan starred as Dr Syn in which 1963 three part mini-series?

78-2) Who was the first sports star to feature in the famous 'I'm going to Disney World!' advertising campaign?

78-3) What is Shades of Green?

78-4) Who are Princess Mira Nova, Booster Sinclair Munchapper and the robot XR?

78-5) Who is Amelia Fieldmouse?

78-6) 'Hawaiian Honeymoon' is the fourth film in which Disney franchise?

78-7) What is the name of King Louie the orang-utan's twin brother?

78-8) Which ride at Tokyo DisneySea is very similar to the Indiana Jones Adventure: Temple of the Forbidden Eye at Disneyland?

78-9) Which classic Disney character's mother is called Hortense?

78-10) Which Mickey Mouse featurette (with a run time of 24 minutes) appeared in cinemas as a support to 'The Rescuers Down Under'?

Answers to Question Set 78

78-1) Patrick McGoohan was 'The Scarecrow of Romney Marsh', a TV mini-series that was edited for theatrical release as 'Dr. Syn, Alias the Scarecrow'.

78-2) Immediately after winning Super Bowl XXI with the New York Giants in January 1987, Phil Simms looked straight at the camera and said 'I'm gonna go to Disney World', for which he was reportedly paid $75,000.

78-3) Shades of Green is a resort hotel at Walt Disney World owned by the U.S. Department of Defense. As such it is primarily reserved for use by U.S. Armed Forces staff and their families. The hotel was previously known as The Golf Resort and also The Disney Inn.

78-4) Mira, Booster and XR are Team Lightyear of Star Command, led by Captain Buzz Lightyear.

78-5) Mickey Mouse's sister is called Amelia Fieldmouse. She is the mother of Morty and Ferdie.

78-6) Hayley Mills reprised both her roles as twin sisters in 'The Parent Trap IV: Hawaiian Honeymoon'.

78-7) King Louie's twin brother is King Larry.

78-8) Tokyo DisneySea's Indiana Jones ride is called Temple of the Crystal Skull.

78-9) Hortense and her husband Quackmore are the parents of Della and Donald Duck.

78-10) Mickey's version of 'The Prince and the Pauper' supported 'The Rescuers Down Under' in cinemas.

Question Set 79

79-1) Which resort hotel at Disneyland Paris takes its name from a legendary frontiersman?

79-2) What kind of animal is Mickey Mouse's nemesis, Peg Leg Pete?

79-3) What were the names of the two girlfriends that Pluto had in a series of short cartoons?

79-4) Which character made appearances in shorts starring Goofy and later Donald before becoming the seventh and final character to be given a series (albeit only two) of starring roles in theatrical short films??

79-5) What are the full names of Donald's three nephews?

79-6) Commander Norah Li Nebulon is the mother of which Disney animated series title character??

79-7) Which animated movie had its World Premiere at the New Orleans Superdome in June 1996?

79-8) What was the first animal to take up residence at Disney's Animal Kingdom park?

79-9) In 1982 Walt Disney World added a new spur to its monorail tracks. Where did this addition serve?

79-10) Where would you find U.B. Bold, U.R. Daring, U.R. Courageous, I.M. Brave, I.B. Hearty and I.M. Fearless?

Answers to Question Set 79

79-1) At Disneyland Paris guests can stay at the Davy Crockett Ranch.

79-2) Peg Leg Pete is a cat.

79-3) Pluto's girlfriends were Fifi the Peke and Dinah the Dachshund.

79-4) Humphrey the Bear was the star of 'Hooked Bear' and 'In the Bag'.

79-5) Huey, Dewey and Louie's full names are Huebert, Deuteronomy and Louis. They are the sons of Donald's sister Della (also known as Dumbella).

79-6) Commander Nebulon's son is 'Lloyd in Space'.

79-7) 'The Hunchback of Notre Dame' premiered in New Orleans.

79-8) On June 12th 1996, Miles the reticulated giraffe became the first animal introduced into the Animal Kingdom. He was closely followed by a female giraffe, Zari, and a group of seven western lowland gorillas.

79-9) The 1982 monorail expansion at Walt Disney World serves EPCOT.

79-10) U.B. Bold, U.R. Daring, U.R. Courageous, I.M. Brave, I.B. Hearty and I.M. Fearless are the names of the Big Thunder Mountain Railroad trains at Walt Disney World.

Question Set 80

80-1) Which movie features a Princess named Kidagakash Nedakh?

80-2) Which Disney character is occasionally seen dressed as Yoda from the 'Star Wars' franchise?

80-3) Which colourful secret agent teddy bear advocates 'three healthy steps' regarding eating, being healthy and exercising on his Disney TV series?

80-4) Where in Disneyland is the Disneyland Dream Suite, the only place that guests can legitimately stay in the park overnight?

80-5) What did Walt Disney contribute to Fox's 1934 comedy movie 'Servants' Entrance'?

80-6) Playing an actor who is mistaken for a killer, Dick van Dyke starred alongside Edward G. Robinson in which 1968 Disney crime comedy?

80-7) What is Walt Disney's Carolwood Barn?

80-8) Neighbour J Jones lives next door to which Disney character?

80-9) Which proposed side street running off Disneyland's Main Street U.S.A. was to have contained a show about the coming of electric power to houses and would eventually lead to the creation of the Carousel of Progress?

80-10) What was the sequel to 'Old Yeller'?

Answers to Question Set 80

80-1) Kidagakash Nedakh (or Kida) is the main female Atlantean in 'Atlantis: The Lost Empire'.

80-2) Stitch dresses as Yoda, and he has the action figures to prove it.

80-3) 'Special Agent Oso' teaches children 'three healthy steps' on his TV show.

80-4) The Disneyland Dream Suite is in the upper level of New Orleans Square in what used to be the Disney Gallery.

80-5) 'Servant's Entrance' was a comedy movie for which the film-makers at Fox asked Walt Disney to provide a section where the star (Janet Gaynor) sings with an animated cutlery set.

80-6) Dick van Dyke and Edward G. Robinson starred in 'Never a Dull Moment'.

80-7) Walt Disney's Carolwood Barn is a museum in Griffiths Park, Los Angeles. It is the actual barn that Walt used as a machine shop while working in his back yard.

80-8) Neighbour J Jones lives next door to Donald Duck in Donald's regular comic strip.

80-9) Edison Square would have been a side street off Main Street U.S.A.

80-10) The follow-up movie told the story of 'Old Yeller's son, 'Savage Sam'.

Question Set 81

81-1) What kind of animal was 'Big Red' in Disney's 1962 adventure movie?

81-2) What is Palo?

81-3) What are the three All Star Resorts at Walt Disney World?

81-4) LeFou is the comedy sidekick of which Disney villain?

81-5) Karen Dotrice and Matthew Garber, who played Jane and Michael Banks in 'Mary Poppins', worked together as children in which other two Disney movies?

81-6) Which TV series features the villains Dr Drakken, Shego, Monkey Fist and Duff Killigan?

81-7) Which sorceress duck frequently plots to steal Scrooge McDuck's Number One Dime?

81-8) For 14 years an a cappella singing group called Four For A Dollar warmed up the audience at which Walt Disney World show?

81-9) Which classic animation movie features the characters Big Chief and Squaw and their daughter, Tiger Lilly?

81-10) What is the name of Brownstone National Park's fussy Park Ranger who is seen in several short films, usually annoying Donald Duck or Humphrey the Bear?

Answers to Question Set 81

81-1) 'Big Red' was an Irish Setter.

81-2) Palo is an adults-only fine dining restaurant aboard the Disney Cruise ships.

81-3) Walt Disney World's three All-Star Resorts are Music, Movies and Sports.

81-4) LeFou (which means 'the fool' in French) is Gaston's maltreated subordinate in 'Beauty and the Beast'.

81-5) Karen Dotrice and Matthew Garber starred in 'The Three Lives of Thomasina' in 1964 and 'The Gnome-Mobile' in 1967.

81-6) Dr Drakken, Shego, Monkey Fist and Duff Killigan are all bad guys from 'Kim Possible'.

81-7) Scrooge McDuck's sorceress nemesis is Magica De Spell.

81-8) The singing group Four For A Dollar (also known as Return To Zero) were the opening act for the Disney's Hollywood Studios stage show of 'Beauty and the Beast'.

81-9) Big Chief, Squaw and Tiger Lilly all appear in the movie 'Peter Pan'.

81-10) Brownstone National Park's Park Ranger is J. Audubon Woodlore.

Question Set 82

82-1) Duke Sigmund Igthorn is the main villain in which Disney animated TV series?

82-2) Who are the stars of the Academy Award-nominated and Christmas-themed short film 'Toy Tinkers'?

82-3) The National Film Board of Canada commissioned a short movie called '7 Wise Dwarfs' (starring the short folk from 'Snow White') to promote what?

82-4) In the 1961 animated movie '101 Dalmatians', to how many puppies does Perdita give birth?

82-5) Who narrates the film in the 'One Man's Dream' exhibit at Disney's Hollywood Studios'?

82-6) Who are Cruella de Ville's inept henchmen in the '101 Dalmatians' franchise?

82-7) Which toy from the 'Toy Story' series makes an appearance in 'Monsters Inc.', when the little girl Boo hands it to Sulley?

82-8) The building where Innoventions is now at Disneyland originally housed the Carousel of Progress, but which attraction was in the same building from 1974 to 1988?

82-9) Which space-age circus / song and dance revue show was planned for the same area as part of Michael Eisner's cancelled Tomorrowland 2055 makeover?

82-10) In a Disney TV animated series, Tino Tonitini, Lorrain McQuarrie, Carver Descartes, and Petratishkovna Katsufrakis are collectively known as what?

Answers to Question Set 82

82-1) Duke Sigmund Igthorn is the bad guy in 'Disney's Adventures of the Gummi Bears'.

82-2) 'Toy Tinkers' starred Donald Duck and Chip an' Dale. It was nominated for the 1950 Best Animated Short Film Oscar but lost out to one of the Loony Tunes series starring Pepé le Pew.

82-3) Doc, Dopey and the others appeared in 1941's '7 Wise Dwarfs' to promote the buying of Canadian war bonds.

82-4) Perdita has 15 puppies.

82-5) Dame Julie Andrews narrates the 'One Man's Dream' movie.

82-6) The bumbling brothers Horace and Jasper Badun worked for Cruella de Ville before going straight and opening their own ladies fashion store.

82-7) Boo gives Sulley her Jessie doll from the 'Toy Story' films.

82-8) America Sings occupied the Carousel Theater in Disneyland between 1974 and 1988.

82-9) George Lucas was involved in the planning of Plectu's Fantastic Intergalactic Revue which, if it had been constructed, would also have been located in the Carousel Theater

82-10) Tino Tonitini, Lor McQuarrie, Carver Descartes, and Tish Katsufrakis are 'The Weekenders'.

Question Set 83

83-1) What is the name of the cat who annoys Pluto in the short films 'Puss-Café', 'Plutopia' and 'Cold Turkey'?

83-2) Which Texan folk hero was the star of a 1947 Disney animation, has a restaurant named after him at Walt Disney World, and was played by Patrick Swayze in a 1995 live action movie?

83-3) Bill Paxton and Charlize Theron starred in Disney's 1998 remake of which 1949 monster movie?

83-4) Which Disney TV series was set in the Tipton hotel in Boston?

83-5) What stage show, based on the 'Dick Tracy' movie, ran at the MGM Studios park and also at Disneyland's Videopolis?

83-6) As well as Bianca in 'The Rescuers' movies, for which other main animation character did Eva Gabor provide the voice?

83-7) Which characters from 'The Lion King' had their own TV series?

83-8) In which movie does Phil Collins play the voice of Lucky?

83-9) Which classic Disney movie was based on the books of English author Mary Norton?

83-10) Between which two countries' pavilions is EPCOT's International Gateway?

Answers to Question Set 83

83-1) Pluto's feline annoyance was called Milton.

83-2) Pecos Bill first appeared in a segment of 'Fun and Fancy Free'. Patrick Swayze played him in the movie 'Tall Tale: The Unbelievable Adventures of Pecos Bill', and the Pecos Bill Tall Tales Inn and Café is at the Magic Kingdom

83-3) Bill Paxton and Charlize Theron starred in 'Mighty Joe Young'.

83-4) 'The Suite Life of Zack and Cody' was set in the Tipton Hotel.

83-5) The theme parks' 'Dick Tracy' show was titled 'Diamond Double-Cross'.

83-6) Eva Gabor was the voice of Duchess in 'The Aristocats'.

83-7) The spin-off TV series from 'The Lion King' was called 'The Lion King's Timon and Pumbaa'. It ran for five successful series.

83-8) Phil Collins voiced 'Lucky' in 'Jungle Book 2'. Lucky is a new vulture introduced in addition to Buzzie, Flaps, Dizzie, & Ziggy from the original movie.

83-9) The source material for 'Bedknobs and Broomsticks' was Mary Norton's novels 'The Magic Bed Knob; or, How to Become a Witch in Ten Easy Lessons' and 'Bonfires and Broomsticks'. Norton is probably best known for having also written 'The Borrowers'.

83-10) Guests entering EPCOT through the International Gateway would arrive in the park between the France and United Kingdom pavilions.

Question Set 84

84-1) What was the sequel to the 1975 movie 'Escape to Witch Mountain' called?

84-2) ... and what TV movie (the pilot for an abandoned TV series) was the third in the 'Witch Mountain' series

84-3) The 1956 movie 'The Great Locomotive Chase', starring Fess Parker and Jeffrey Hunter, was set during which war?

84-4) Tokyo Disneyland is actually situated in which town in Tokyo Bay?

84-5) What is the name of Mickey's theme tune that begins with the lines, 'I'm the guy they call little Mickey Mouse, Got a sweetie down in the chicken house'?

84-6) In the 'Toy Story' movies, what is the name of Andy's dog?

84-7) Which themed land in the Disney California Adventure Park is meant to resemble a 1940s airfield?

84-8) Disneyland Paris is situated in which town, some 30 kilometers away from the city of Paris?

84-9) Reese Witherspoon walks across the Kalahari Desert to escape African poachers in which 1993?

84-10) Which interactive exhibit about nutrition, exercise and healthy eating at EPCOT was closed within a few weeks of its soft opening in 2012 due to complaints from the National Association to Advance Fat Acceptance, among others?

Answers to Question Set 84

84-1) Bette Davis and Christopher Lee starred in 'Return From Witch Mountain' in 1978.

84-2) The Witch Mountain TV movie from 1982 was called 'Beyond Witch Mountain'.

84-3) 'The Great Locomotive Chase' was set during the American Civil War.

84-4) Tokyo Disneyland was built on land reclaimed from Tokyo Bay in the town of Urayasu.

84-5) Mickey's theme tune is called 'Minnie's Yoo Hoo'.

84-6) Andy's dog is a dachshund called Buster.

84-7) Condor Flats resembles a 1940s airfield.

84-8) Disneyland Paris is actually in the town of Marne-la-Vallée, almost 20 miles outside of Paris.

84-9) Reese Witherspoon appeared in 'A Far Off Place'.

84-10) Habit Heroes, which featured animated fitness superheroes Will Power and Callie Stenics and oversized villains The Glutton, Snacker and Lead Bottom, was closed shortly after opening due to claims that it was seen as bullying and shaming overweight people.

Question Set 85

85-1) In 'Oliver and Company', what kind of creature is Oliver?

85-2) What is the real life sporting event depicted in Disney's 2004 live action movie, 'Miracle'?

85-3) Denahi and Sitka are brothers of the main character in which animated movie?

85-4) Which 30 minute documentary film was shot at the same time as, and covers similar themes to, 'Saludos Amigos'?

85-5) The earliest Pixar short films were collected together as which home VHS?

85-6) Which 2008 family comedy movie had Jamie Lee Curtis worrying about her pet dog, which had fallen into the clutches of an evil Doberman named El Diablo?

85-7) Who were Luath, Bodger and Tao?

85-8) Which classic Disney character has been voiced by Pinto Colvig, George Johnson and Bill Farmer?

85-9) Which movie legend provided the narration for Disney's 2004 natural history documentary 'Sacred Planet'?

85-10) Jenny Agutter played which title character in a 1981 drama about a woman who leaves her domineering husband to teach in a school for the deaf?

Answers to Question Set 85

85-1) Oliver is an orphaned kitten.

85-2) 'Miracle' told the story of the USA ice hockey team's victory over the USSR in the 1980 Winter Olympics.

85-3) Denahi and Sitka are Kenai's brothers in 'Brother Bear'.

85-4) 'South of the Border with Disney' was filmed on the same South American trip as 'Saludos Amigos'.

85-5) The earliest Pixar short films were brought together as 'Tiny Toy Stories'.

85-6) Jamie Lee Curtis was the human star of 'Beverly Hills Chihuahua'.

85-7) Luath was the Labrador, Bodger the Bull Terrier and Tao was the Siamese cat in the 1963 movie 'The Incredible Journey'.

85-8) Pinto Colvig, George Johnson and Bill Farmer have all provided the voice of Goofy.

85-9) Robert Redford narrated 'Sacred Planet'.

85-10) Jenny Agutter starred as 'Amy'.

Question Set 86

86-1) 'The Shnookums and Meat Funny Cartoon Show' was a spin-off from which other Disney TV series?

86-2) Where would you find José, Pierre, Michael and Fritz?

86-3) Which 1994 sporting comedy starring Danny Glover, Tony Danza and Christopher Lloyd, was a remake of a 1951 MGM movie by the same name?

86-4) What is Minnie Mouse's full name?

86-5) Disney distributes English language versions of films made by which Japanese studio, whose movies have included 'Spirited Away' and 'Howl's Moving Castle'?

86-6) Which circle-vision movie attraction has also been presented around the world under the names From Time to Time, Un Voyage à Travers le Temps and Visionarium?

86-7) The songs Three Cheers for Everything, Turn On the Old Music Box and I'm a Happy-Go-Lucky Fellow were written for – but not used in – which animated movie?

86-8) Who was the last of the original Mouseketeers selected to be on the show, and the only one to be discovered by Walt Disney himself?

86-9) Which two birds took ownership of The Enchanted Tiki Room in Walt Disney World's 'Under New Management' version of the attraction?

86-10) What is 'Kya Mast Hai Life'?

Answers to Question Set 86

86-1) 'The Shnookums and Meat Funny Cartoon Show' was a spin-off from 'Marsupilami'.

86-2) José, Pierre, Michael and Fritz are the four parrots in the original version of Walt Disney's Enchanted Tiki Room.

86-3) Danny Glover, Tony Danza and Christopher Lloyd starred in Disney's remake of 'Angels in the Outfield'.

86-4) Minnie is a shortened form of Minerva Mouse.

86-5) Disney distributes Studio Ghibli movies.

86-6) From Time to Time, Un Voyage à Travers le Temps and Visionarium operated in Walt Disney World's Tomorrowland as The Timekeeper.

86-7) Three Cheers for Everything, Turn On the Old Music Box and I'm a Happy-Go-Lucky Fellow were originally written for 'Pinocchio'. Jiminy Cricket finally got to sing I'm a Happy-Go-Lucky Fellow in 'Fun and Fancy Free'.

86-8) The final person chosen to be an original Mouseketeer was Annette Funicello.

86-9) The Enchanted Tiki Room: 'Under New Management' was run by Iago from 'Aladdin' and Zazu from 'The Lion King'.

86-10) 'Kya Mast Hai Life' is a popular teen TV series from India's Disney Channel.

Question Set 87

87-1) Bruce Willis has to look after an eight year old version of himself in which family movie from 2000?

87-2) Which two audio-animatronic shows previously occupied the space in EPCOT's The Land pavilion where Soarin' is now?

87-3) 'Myth of the White Wolf' was the subtitle of which 1991 film's sequel?

87-4) Who provides the voice for the Ant Queen in 'A Bug's Life'?

87-5) Which live action musical was the last movie that Walt Disney personally worked on?

87-6) What is the name of 'Aladdin's father?

87-7) Which of Disney's theme parks is the largest?

87-8) Which character's name means magnolia in her native language?

87-9) Which 1943 Disney short film is a chilling piece of propaganda showing a German boy being raised to fight for the Nazis?

87-10) Down to Earth, an Oscar-nominated song by Peter Gabriel, features in which Pixar movie?

Answers to Question Set 87

87-1) Bruce Willis was the star of 'Disney's The Kid'.

87-2) On EPCOT Center's grand opening day in 1982, The Land included a show called Kitchen Kabaret. This was replaced in 1994 with Food Rocks which itself would later give way to the Soarin' ride.

87-3) The sequel to 'White Fang' was called 'White Fang 2: Myth of the White Wolf'.

87-4) 'A Bug's Life's Queen is voiced by Phyllis Diller.

87-5) Walt's last film was 'The Happiest Millionaire'.

87-6) 'Aladdin's father, Casim, first appeared in 'Aladdin and the King of Thieves'.

87-7) At more than 500 acres (202 ha), Disney's Animal Kingdom is the company's largest theme park.

87-8) 'Mulan' literally translates as magnolia or wood-orchid.

87-9) 'Education for Death: The Making of a Nazi' is possibly the strongest propaganda movie to come from the Disney studio during World War II.

87-10) The song Down to Earth appears in 'WALL-E'.

Question Set 88

88-1) According to the title of its feature length spin-off, why were Disney characters trapped in the 'House of Mouse' club?

88-2) Which Disney film was shown to over 100,000,000 American schoolgirls during their health education classes?

88-3) A show called 'The Days of Swine and Roses' performed daily at Walt Disney World from 1991 to 1995. Where was it, and who were its stars?

88-4) The four major divisions of the Walt Disney Company are Consumer Products, Media Network, Studio Entertainment and what other?

88-5) Which actor played Quasimodo in 'The Hunchback of Notre Dame' and its sequel?

88-6) According to Lilo, what does the Hawaiian word 'Ohana' mean?

88-7) Who are Lucky, Thunder, Rolly, Patch, Pepper, Dipstick, Penny, Cadpig, Freckles, Jewel, and Fidget?

88-8) Which two animators – two of Walt's famous 'Nine Old Men' – were so well respected that the mad scientist in Mickey's 1995 short film 'Runaway Brain' was named after them? They were also given animated cameos in Warner Brothers' 'The Iron Giant' and Pixar's 'The Incredibles'.

88-9) Who can be found standing in a fountain in Disney's Hollywood Studios dressed in a Statue of Liberty costume?

88-10) Who is Flintheart Glomgold?

Answers to Question Set 88

88-1) The TV show's first movie spin-off was called 'Mickey's Magical Christmas: Snowed in at the House of Mouse'.

88-2) In 1946 Disney animators produced the educational 10 minute cartoon, 'The Story of Menstruation'. It was distributed to schools across America.

88-3) The Muppets appeared in 'The Days of Swine and Roses' on the New York Street section of MGM Studios.

88-4) The four major divisions of the Walt Disney Company are Consumer Products, Media Network, Studio Entertainment and Theme Parks and Resorts.

88-5) Tom Hulce was the voice of Quasimodo.

88-6) Lilo says that, 'Ohana means family, family means nobody gets left behind. Or forgotten.'

88-7) Lucky, Thunder, Rolly, Patch, Pepper, Dipstick, Penny, Cadpig, Freckles, Jewel, and Fidget are just some of the puppies in '101 Dalmatians'.

88-8) The mad scientist in 'Runaway Brain' was called Dr Frankenollie, after Disney Legends Frank Thomas and Ollie Johnson

88-9) Miss Piggy is the Statue of Liberty.

88-10) Flintheart Glomgold is the Second Richest Duck in the World, and one of Scrooge McDuck's main rivals.

Question Set 89

89-1) How many of the Seven Dwarfs wear glasses?

89-2) Stormalong Bay is a recreation pool at which Walt Disney World resort?

89-3) Which classic Disney live action movie features the characters Professor Pierre M. Aronnax, his assistant, Conseil, and a cocky sailor named Ned Land?

89-4) Where is the only AAA Five Diamond restaurant in Central Florida?

89-5) Which comedian provides the voice for King Fergus in 'Brave'?

89-6) Which 1953 live action movie was shown on U.S. TV in 1956 as a two-part mini-series called 'When Knighthood was in Flower'?

89-7) Which character, appearing in the very first episode of the 1960s 'Walt Disney's Wonderful World of Color' TV series, was Disney's first cartoon character devised specifically for television?

89-8) In 2007, Disneyland's long-closed Submarine Voyage reopened with theming based on which animated movie?

89-9) The pirate crew members Sharky and Bones appear in which Disney Junior series set in the world of Peter Pan?

89-10) A model of which aircraft can be seen bursting out of the Taste Pilots' Grill restaurant at Disney's California Adventure?

Answers to Question Set 89

89-1) Doc is the only dwarf who needs glasses.

89-2) Stormalong Bay is at Disney's Yacht Club resort.

89-3) Professor Pierre M. Aronnax, Conseil and Ned Land all appear in '20,000 Leagues Under the Sea'.

89-4) Central Florida's only AAA Five Diamond restaurant is Victoria and Albert's at Walt Disney World's Grand Floridian Resort & Spa

89-5) Billy Connolly voices 'Brave's King Fergus.

89-6) 'The Sword and the Rose' was shown on TV under the name of the book on which it was based, 'When Knighthood was in Flower'.

89-7) Ludwig von Drake was Disney's first cartoon character created for television.

89-8) Disneyland's Submarine Voyage reopened as Finding Nemo Submarine Voyage.

89-9) Sharky and Bones are members of Captain Hook's crew in 'Jake and the Never Land Pirates'.

89-10) The aeroplane crashing through the wall of the Taste Pilots' Grill is the Bell X1, nicknamed Glamorous Glennis by its pilot, Chuck Yeager. It was in this plane that Yeager made the first manned supersonic flight on October 14, 1947, an event referenced by many tiny details throughout Condor Flats at Disney's California Adventure.

Question Set 90

90-1) For what was Walt Disney posthumously inducted into America's National Inventor's Hall of Fame in 2000?

90-2) Which character in 'Fantasia', though never named in the movie, is usually referred to as Hop Low?

90-3) How many different random ride options are there in Star Tours: The Adventure Continues?

90-4) In which live action movie, based on the novels of Herminie Templeton Kavanagh, did Albert Sharpe play the title character?

90-5) Which Disney Channel Original Movie starred Corbin Bleu as a boxer who discovers a love of jumping rope (skipping)?

90-6) Despite having a successful series of films, which Disney character's television series was cancelled after just five episodes?

90-7) What is the full name of the dark ride featuring characters from 'Pinocchio'?

90-8) The stars of 'Spin and Marty' and 'Zorro' appeared in which 1960 movie about a boy who runs away to join the circus?

90-9) E. Cardon Walker, Bob Graham and William Ellinghouse all spoke at which theme park's opening ceremony?

90-10) Which animated movie formed the basis of the PlayStation game 'Battle at Procyon'?

Answers to Question Set 90

90-1) Walt was inducted into the National Inventor's Hall of Fame for creating the multiplane camera.

90-2) Hop Low is the small dancing mushroom in 'Fantasia's Nutcracker Suite segment who cannot remember his steps.

90-3) Each run of Star Tours: The Adventure Continues delivers one of 54 different film combinations.

90-4) Albert Sharpe played the title role in 'Darby O'Gill and the Little People'.

90-5) Corbin Bleu boxes and jumps rope in 'Jump In!'.

90-6) 'Herbie The Love Bug' was a flop on TV.

90-7) 'Pinocchio' forms the basis for 'Pinocchio's Daring Journey'.

90-8) 'Toby Tyler' ran away to the circus.

90-9) Card Walker was Disney's Chairman and CEO, Bob Graham was Florida Governor and William Ellinghouse was the chairman of sponsors AT&T at the time of EPCOT's opening.

90-10) 'Battle at Procyon' took place after the events shown in 'Treasure Planet'.

Question Set 91

91-1) Dance sequences from 'Snow White and the Seven Dwarfs', 'The Jungle Book' and 'The Aristocats' were reused for the animation of which movie?

91-2) Where is Walt Disney World's only microbrewery?

91-3) Which 1962 space comedy starring Tom Tryon and Edmund O'Brien caused the F.B.I. to complain to Disney?

91-4) Which animated TV series, starring Donald and teenage versions of his nephews, was originally to have been aired under the title 'Duck Daze'?

91-5) In the 'Haunted Mansion' movie, what character does Terence Stamp play?

91-6) Which animated movie has Linda Hunt, Billy Connolly and Christian Bale voicing minor characters?

91-7) Why does Eddie Murphy, as Mushu in 'Mulan', say that he 'don't do that tongue thing'?

91-8) The teen hangout areas in the fake forward funnels of the Disney Magic and Disney Wonder originally housed what sports club that featured multiple TV screens broadcasting all the latest sports news and events from around the world?

91-9) Where is Mount Prometheus?

91-10) Which 'Toy Story' character has his own Zigzag Spin ride in Disney's parks in Paris and Hong Kong?

Answers to Question Set 91

91-1) Disney animators noticeably copied many frames from previous movies in the production of 'Robin Hood'.

91-2) The Big River Grille and Brewing Works brews beer at Walt Disney World's Boardwalk.

91-3) The F.B.I. took exception to their agents being portrayed in "a most slapstick and uncomplimentary manner" in 'Moon Pilot'.

91-4) Late in its production 'Duck Daze' was retitled 'Quack Pack'.

91-5) Terence Stamp stars as Ramsley, Master Gracey's butler, in 'The Haunted Mansion'.

91-6) Linda Hunt, Billy Connolly and Christian Bale all had voice roles in 'Pocahontas'.

91-7) Mushu is upset that Mulan could think he is a mere lizard and complains, 'Hey! Dragon. *Dra-gon*, not lizard. I don't do that tongue thing'.

91-8) The highest points of the Disney Magic and Disney Wonder were originally the ESPN Skybox sports bars.

91-9) Mount Prometheus is the huge volcanic centrepiece of Tokyo DisneySea.

91-10) The Disneylands in Paris and Hong Kong both feature Slinky Dog Zigzag Spin rides aimed at smaller children.

Question Set 92

92-1) Which loveable rascal is the son of 'Lady and the Tramp'?

92-2) Who are Burger, Baggy, Bouncer, Bigtime, Bankjob, and Babyface?

92-3) Which two professional baseball teams contested the opening game at the Wide World of Sports Complex in March 1997?

92-4) Which animated TV series began with a feature length TV movie called 'Plunder and Lightning'?

92-5) What is the name of the raccoon in 'Pocahontas'?

92-6) Which animated character occasionally takes on the costume and secret identity of Papernik?

92-7) 'Back in the Habit' was the sequel to which 1993 comedy movie?

92-8) Which 1992 short film tells the fictional story of how Mickey Mouse came to Hollywood and was discovered by Walt Disney?

92-9) ... and who played the part of Walt in that movie?

92-10) Which acting superstar was the voice of 'Bolt'?

Answers to Question Set 92

92-1) Lady and Tramp's son is called Scamp.

92-2) Burger, Baggy, Bouncer, Bigtime, Bankjob, and Babyface are some of the notorious Beagle Boys criminal gang.

92-3) The first game to be played at the Wide World of Sports complex was between the Atlanta Braves and the Cincinnati Reds.

92-4) 'Plunder and Lightning' was the introductory movie for the series 'TaleSpin'.

92-5) Pocahontas's raccoon friend is called Meeko.

92-6) Donald Duck took on the role of Papernik after finding the diary and costume of the late gentleman burglar and vigilante Phantom Duck.

92-7) 'Sister Act 2' was subtitled 'Back in the Habit'.

92-8) 'Mickey's Audition' showed Mickey's arrival in Hollywood from his own point of view.

92-9) In 'Mickey's Audition', Roy E. Disney appeared as his Uncle Walt.

92-10) John Travolta provided the voice for 'Bolt'.

Question Set 93

93-1) A screenplay entitled 'Toon Platoon' was produced as an intended sequel to which movie?

93-2) Which songwriters produced music and lyrics for 'Beauty and the Beast', 'Aladdin' and 'The Little Mermaid'?

93-3) Which ride replaced Superstar Limo at Disney's California Adventure?

93-4) Comic artist Mike Mignola (of Hellboy fame) provided the artistic look and feel of which Disney animation?

93-5) What kind of creature does a young Canadian boy converse with in a 1975 Disney live action movie?

93-6) In the animated 'Alice in Wonderland', what does the Queen of Hearts use as a mallet and ball when playing croquet?

93-7) Who was the first President of the Walt Disney Company who wasn't a member of the Disney family?

93-8) The singer Helen Reddy made her only starring role in which Disney movie?

93-9) Who were Stanley (blue), Ozzie (green), Tippi (pink), Dink (red) and Bink (peach)?

93-10) The sequel to which classic animation was subtitled 'Dreams Come True'?

Answers to Question Set 93

93-1) Had it ever gone into production, 'Toon Platoon' would have shown Roger Rabbit's early years and his adventures in World War II.

93-2) Academy Award winners Howard Ashman and Alan Menken collaborated on some of Disney's most memorable songs of the late 'eighties and early 'nineties.

93-3) The unpopular Superstar Limo was replaced in 2006 by Monsters Inc. Mike and Sulley to the Rescue.

93-4) Mike Mignola was production designer on 'Atlantis: The Lost Empire'.

93-5) A young Canadian was 'The Boy Who Talked to Badgers'.

93-6) The Queen of Hearts plays croquet with a flamingo and a hedgehog.

93-7) Donn B. Tatum succeeded Roy O. Disney as company President, Chairman and C.E.O.

93-8) Helen Reddy starred in 'Pete's Dragon'.

93-9) Stanley, Ozzie, Tippi, Dink and Bink were 'Disney's Fluppy Dogs'.

93-10) In 2002 Disney released 'Cinderella II: Dreams Come True'.

Question Set 94

94-1) Jan-Michael Vincent (of 'Airwolf' fame) played a Tarzan-like character brought to an American college in the hopes of turning him into a track and field star in which 1973 comedy drama?

94-2) In Walt Disney World's The Many Adventures of Winnie the Pooh ride, who can be seen presenting the deeds of the building to Pooh's friend Owl?

94-3) The logo of which Disney company is an iceberg which looks a lot like Cinderella's castle?

94-4) What was the subtitle of the third Cinderella animated movie?

94-5) In 2009 Disney's Hyperion Books published 'Miles to Go', the autobiography of which actress?

94-6) On which classic non-Disney movie did Imagineer Harper Goff base much of the design of Disney's Jungle Cruise attraction?

94-7) Which theme park has the lowest attendance figures of any of Disney's eleven major parks worldwide?

94-8) Mother Gothel is the villain in which animated movie?

94-9) Who wrote the 'Tarzan' novels?

94-10) ...and which Disney live action movie from 2012 is based on another series of books by the same author?

Answers to Question Set 94

94-1) Jan-Michael Vincent was 'The World's Greatest Athlete'.

94-2) Owl receives the deeds to the Many Adventures of Winnie the Pooh ride building from Mr Toad in a reference to Mr Toad's Wild Ride, the attraction that was previously housed in the same building.

94-3) Disneynature's logo resembles Cinderella's castle.

94-4) In 2007 Disney released 'Cinderella III: A Twist in Time'.

94-5) 'Miles to Go' is the autobiography of Miley Cyrus.

94-6) Harper Goff wanted guests on the Jungle Cruise to think they'd stepped onto the set (and deck) of The African Queen.

94-7) The Walt Disney Studios Park, Disney's second Parisian theme park, has the dubious distinction of the company's least visited park?

94-8) Gothel appears in 'Tangled'.

94-9) Disney's 'Tarzan' was loosely based on the book Tarzan of the Apes by Edgar Rice Burroughs. He also wrote some twenty-five other stories featuring the same character.

94-10) Edgar Rice Burroughs also wrote a series of novels featuring 'John Carter'.

Question Set 95

95-1) Which 1980 comedy movie included Michael J Fox's first film role?

95-2) Which animated Disney TV series was subtitled 'The Goliath Chronicles' for its third and final season?

95-3) Which 1980 live action musical comic strip adaptation starred Robin Williams and Shelley Duvall?

95-4) A 'midget' version of which original Disneyland attraction was introduced to the park two years after opening day?

95-5) Tom Cruise, John Travolta, Leonard Nimoy, Steve Martin, Bob Hope, Dorothy Lamour, Jane Russell, Harrison Ford, Tony Curtis and many others have all left what at Disney's Hollywood Studios?

95-6) For what did Peter Scolari take over from Rick Moranis as Dr Wayne Szalinski?

95-7) In which film would you find the characters Zira and her son, Kovu?

95-8) Which creatures appear in the 'Fantasia 2000' segment based around The Pines of Rome by Ottorino Respighi?

95-9) What was the title of the sequel to the Nicolas Cage movie, 'National Treasure'?

95-10) Which daytime show on and over the lagoon at EPCOT featured biplanes and dragonboats?

Answers to Question Set 95

95-1) Michael J Fox's film debut was 'Midnight Madness', released two years before his breakthrough role in 'Family Ties'.

95-2) The third season of 'Gargoyles' was subtitled 'The Goliath Chronicles'.

95-3) Robin Williams and Shelley Duvall starred in 'Popeye', a co-production between Disney and Paramount.

95-4) Autopia gave guests the chance to drive in slot cars at Disneyland on its 1955 opening day. Junior Autopia was added a year later and Midget Autopia in 1957. Midget Autopia operated until 1966 when the entire ride was transferred to the Walt Disney Municipal Park in Marceline, Missouri.

95-5) Many actors have left their handprints in the cement outside The Great Movie Ride.

95-6) Peter Scolari played Wayne Szalinski in three seasons of 'Honey I Shrunk the Kids: The TV Show'.

95-7) Zira and Kovu appear in 'The Lion King II: Simba's Pride'.

95-8) The Pines of Rome is the soundtrack to the flying whales segment of 'Fantasia 2000'.

95-9) 'National Treasure's sequel was titled 'National Treasure: Book of Secrets'.

95-10) Biplanes and dragonboats played a large part in EPCOT's Skylaidescope show which ran from 1985 to 1987. The planes involved were launched from the nearby EPCOT Center Ultralight Flightpark.

Question Set 96

96-1) What is 'The Golden Mickeys'?

96-2) Name Simba's parents in 'The Lion King'.

96-3) The 1992 Indian movie, 'Chamatkar' about a sports coach who can talk to a dead gangster, was based on which 1962 Disney family comedy?

96-4) The singer Debbie Gibson has played which Disney role on Broadway?

96-5) What was the first official crossover between the two companies after Disney acquired the Marvel Comics Group?

96-6) The songs You Think You Blink, Lead the Righteous Life, West Wind, The Eyes of Love and The Chimpanzoo were among those written for which movie although they were all dropped before the final version?

96-7) The lead character in Universal's 1972 sci-fi movie 'Silent Running' nicknamed his three small service robots after which cartoon characters?

96-8) Where at Walt Disney World could you have seen live improvisational comedy from The AnaComical Players?

96-9) Which 'Aladdin' character has the nickname 'Little Bobo'?

96-10) Which roles do Minnie Mouse and Daisy Duck play in 2004's 'The Three Musketeers'?

Answers to Question Set 96

96-1) 'The Golden Mickeys' is a stage show which has been performed on board the Disney Cruise Line ships and also at Hong Kong Disneyland. It takes the form of an Oscar awards ceremony revue show.

96-2) Simba's parents are called Mufasa and Sarabi.

96-3) 'Chamatkar' was a loose remake of Disney's 'Blackbeard's Ghost'.

96-4) Debbie Gibson played Belle in the Broadway production of 'Beauty and the Beast' in 1997 & 1998.

96-5) Wayne and Lanny from 'Prep and Landing' starred in a short story called 'Mansion: Impossible' with the superhero team, The Avengers.

96-6) You Think You Blink, Lead the Righteous Life, West Wind, The Eyes of Love and The Chimpanzoo were all written for the 'Mary Poppins' film.

96-7) In 'Silent Running', Lowell nicknames his robots Huey, Dewey and Louie.

96-8) The AnaComical Players used to appear at EPCOT's Wonders of Life pavilion.

96-9) In the 'Aladdin' TV series, the Sultan revealed his nickname: Little Bobo.

96-10) In 'The Three Musketeers' Minnie plays the role of the Princess of France while Daisy is her lady in waiting.

Question Set 97

97-1) Who does Monsieur D'Arque imprison in his asylum, the Maison Des Lunes?

97-2) Jim Dale played Jasper Bloodshy in which 1978 comedy western?

97-3) Which attraction was demolished to make room for the construction of Mission: Space at EPCOT?

97-4) Which 2011 live action movie is about a High School class president trying to find a venue for the end of year dance after the original location is vandalised?

97-5) 'A Sitch in Time' and 'So the Drama' are feature length spin-offs from which TV series?

97-6) In which beloved Touchstone movie does Edward Lewis fall in love with Vivian Ward?

97-7) Which Disney Channel sitcom features a musical prodigy, a girl with a photographic memory and a young artist at a San Francisco school for those with Advanced Natural Talents?

97-8) Which surfer-themed restaurant served pizzas and pasta dishes throughout Disney's California Adventure's first decade?

97-9) Julie Kavner is famous for being the voice of Marge Simpson but whose animated mother did she voice for Disney?

97-10) Who was Minnie Moo?

Answers to Question Set 97

97-1) Belle's father, Maurice, is taken away by Monsieur D'Arque in 'Beauty and the Beast'. In the stage show version he gets to sing a song with Gaston and LeFou called 'The Maison Des Lunes' – the house of lunatics.

97-2) Jim Dale played Jasper Bloodshy in 'Hot Lead and Cold Feet'.

97-3) Mission: Space replaced Horizons at EPCOT.

97-4) In 2011 Disney released a movie about a group of teenagers preparing for their 'Prom'.

97-5) 'Kim Possible' is the star of the TV movies 'A Sitch in Time' and 'So the Drama'.

97-6) Edward Lewis and Vivian Ward were played by Richard Gere and Julia Roberts in 'Pretty Woman'.

97-7) Children with Advanced Natural Talents are recruited into the 'A.N.T. Farm'.

97-8) Disney's California Adventure's pizza restaurant was called Pizza Oom Mow Mow.

97-9) As well as voicing Marge Simpson, Julie Kavner was the voice of Timon's Ma in 'Lion King1½'.

97-10) Minnie Moo was a live Holstein cow with a unique 'Hidden Mickey' black mark on her white flank. She spent most of her fifteen years being petted by guests at Walt Disney World.

Question Set 98

98-1) Which classic theme park attraction has had incarnations at Tokyo Disneyland called Stitch Presents Aloha e Komo Mai! and Get the Fever?

98-2) What is the name of Goofy's seldom-seen uncle who is very similar in character and appearance to Donald's uncle Ludwig von Drake?

98-3) What kind of bird does Russell think that Kevin is in 'Up'?

98-4) Before its rebranding in 2010, what was the previous name of the ESPN Wide World of Sports Complex?

98-5) Had it ever come to fruition, what would Disneyland's version of the Indiana Jones stunt show have been called?

98-6) What is the name of the scheming butler in 'The Aristocats'?

98-7) Disney based their 1979 comedy 'Unidentified Flying Oddball' on Mark Twain's A Connecticut Yankee in King Arthur's Court. What was the movie's alternate title?

98-8) What is the name of the Disney Vacation Club annex to the Contemporary Resort at Walt Disney World?

98-9) Which famous long distance runner was the subject of the 1999 docudrama movie 'Endurance'?

98-10) Which animated character is the mascot of the University of Oregon's sports teams?

Answers to Question Set 98

98-1) Tokyo Disneyland's Enchanted Tiki Room has been presented in several unique versions.

98-2) Goofy's scientist uncle is the implausibly named Ludwig von Goof.

98-3) Russell thinks that Kevin is a snipe, even though Kevin looks nothing like one.

98-4) Disney's Wide World of Sports Complex was renamed ESPN Wide World of Sports.

98-5) After the success of the Indiana Jones Epic Stunt Spectacular at the MGM Studios at Florida, plans were made for a Young Indiana Jones and the Adventure Spectacular show featuring a teenage version of the hero.

98-6) The butler in 'The Aristocats' is called Edgar Balthazar.

98-7) 'Unidentified Flying Oddball' was also released as 'The Spaceman and King Arthur'.

98-8) Bay Lake Tower opened as part of the Contemporary Resort in 2009.

98-9) Ethiopian runner Haile Gebrselassie played himself in 'Endurance'.

98-10) University of Oregon's mascot is based on Donald Duck.

Question Set 99

99-1) The character Dave Stutler is the hero in which 2010 live action movie?

99-2) Which Disney Channel sketch series is a spin-off from 'Sonny With A Chance'?

99-3) Which film is partially set on the Buy n' Large (BnL) Starliner Axiom?

99-4) Which TV series starring Hulk Hogan and Terry Lemon was filmed at the Disney-MGM studios and throughout Walt Disney World? It ran for just one season in 1994.

99-5) What was the subtitle of the second movie in the Princess Diaries series?

99-6) What damage to herself does 'Pollyanna' do when she falls from a tree?

99-7) Who are Aunt Arctic, The Penguin Band, Rockhopper, Sensei, Rookie, Gary, and Cadence?

99-8) Who starred as 'Mr Magoo' in Disney's live action movie?

99-9) Which 2011 live action sequel features a mermaid called Syrena?

99-10) In a classic Mickey Mouse short film, what kind of animal escapes from the zoo and joins Mickey in his bathtub?

Answers to Question Set 99

99-1) Jay Baruchel plays Dave Stutler in 'The Sorcerer's Apprentice'.

99-2) 'So Random!' was originally a show-within-a-show section of 'Sonny With A Chance'.

99-3) 'WALL-E's human characters are aboard the BnL Starliner Axiom.

99-4) Disney's Grand Floridian, Old Key West, Fort Wilderness Campground and EPCOT's Living Seas were among the locations used for filming 'Thunder in Paradise'.

99-5) Anne Hathaway and Julie Andrews reprised their roles in 'The Princess Diaries 2: Royal Engagement'.

99-6) 'Pollyanna's fall results in her losing the use of her legs.

99-7) Aunt Arctic, The Penguin Band, Rockhopper, Sensei, Rookie, Gary, and Cadence are all characters from the 'Club Penguin' franchise.

99-8) Leslie Nielsen was 'Mr Magoo' in 1997.

99-9) Syrena appears in 'Pirates of the Caribbean: On Stranger Tides'.

99-10) Mickey Mouse finds his bathtub is inhabited by Salty the Seal in 1948's 'Mickey and the Seal'.

Question Set 100

100-1) What was the actor Patrick McGoohan's final role before his death?

100-2) What Disney Channel animated series features a Suburban Daredevil?

100-3) Since 1981, Feld Entertainment have toured the globe with over thirty shows under which collective name?

100-4) According to Tim Burton's 2010 'Alice in Wonderland', what is the name of the dormouse?

100-5) At what sport was Walt's nephew, Roy E. Disney, a record-breaking participant?

100-6) Who is the official Godmother of the Disney Wonder cruise ship?

100-7) Walt Disney World's Magic Kingdom, Disneyland in California and Tokyo Disneyland all include the Rivers of America. What are the equivalent rivers at Paris and Hong Kong called?

100-8) Chevy Chase, Farrah Fawcett and Jonathan Taylor Thomas starred in which 1995 Disney comedy about a boy coming to terms with his new potential stepfather?

100-9) Artist Mary Blair was responsible for the overall design of which classic Disney attraction?

100-10) Which animated TV series was about a dog called Spot who disguised himself as a boy and attended school under the name of Scott Leadready II?

Answers to Question Set 100

100-1) Patrick McGoohan's last role was as the voice of Billy Bones in 'Treasure Planet'.

100-2) The full title of the Disney XD's first original animated series was 'Kick Buttowski: Suburban Daredevil'.

100-3) Feld Entertainment produces the Disney On Ice shows.

100-4) The dormouse in 'Alice in Wonderland' is named Mallymkun.

100-5) Roy E. Disney held many sailing speed records.

100-6) Tinker Bell is the Disney Wonder's Godmother.

100-7) While the American and Japanese parks feature Rivers of America, Paris has the Rivers of the Far West and Hong Kong has Rivers of Adventure.

100-8) Chevy Chase, Farrah Fawcett and Jonathan Taylor Thomas starred in 'Man of the House'.

100-9) Mary Blair is probably most famous for designing It's A Small World.

100-10) Spot became Scott in 'Teacher's Pet'.

If you enjoyed 'The World's Toughest Disney Quiz Book' then search for 'The Daily Disney Quiz' blog subscription by Shaun Finnie on Amazon. It's a daily mailing of more questions like these.

Shaun Finnie is also the author of 'The Disneylands that Never Were'.

www.shaunfinnie.com

12748419R00120

Printed in Poland
by Amazon Fulfillment
Poland Sp. z o.o., Wrocław